TABLE OF CONTENTS

How Do I Let Go?
Coping With Life's Changes Both Good and Bad
©Copyright 2013 by Dr. Harry Jay

DISCLAIMER AND TERMS OF USE AGREEMENT:

(Please Read This Before Using This Book)

This information is for educational and informational purposes only. The content is not intended to be a substitute for any professional advice, diagnosis, or treatment.

The author and publisher of this book and the accompanying materials have used their best efforts in preparing this book.

The author and publisher make no representation or warranties with respect to the accuracy, applicability, fitness, or completeness of the contents of this book. The information contained in this book is strictly for educational purposes. Therefore, if you wish to apply ideas contained in this book, you are taking full responsibility for your actions.

The author and publisher disclaim any warranties (express or implied), merchantability, or fitness for any particular purpose. The author and publisher shall in no event be held liable to any party for any direct, indirect, punitive, special, incidental or other consequential damages arising directly or indirectly from any use of this material, which is provided "as is", and without warranties. As always, the advice of a competent legal, tax, accounting, medical or other professional should be sought where applicable.

The author and publisher do not warrant the performance, effectiveness or applicability of any sites listed or linked to in this book. All links are for information purposes only and are not warranted for content, accuracy or any other implied or explicit purpose. No part of this may be copied, or changed in any format, or used in any way other than what is outlined within this course under any circumstances. Violators will be prosecuted.

Introduction

I have been a behavioral scientist for over 31-years. I am also a research scientist for Applied Mind Sciences.

In human mind research, we attempt to understand why people do the things they do but more importantly, we seek to understand why people DO NOT do what they are supposed to do.

Letting go of relationships, things, stuff and maladies are just a few things people have trouble letting go of and releasing from their lives. So we will discuss in detail how to let go and what not to hold on to in the first place.

I have written over 200-books published on Amazon alone but this book is one of the most important ones I will write. The subject matter hits very close to home personally.

Everybody on the planet has loved and lost. In my personal life I lost a wife, a daughter to a drunk driver, friendships, material goods, money and more. This must sound familiar to many of you!

To begin addressing the subject of letting go, it will be necessary to give you some background information regarding the human mind.

Forgive me in advance for being overly verbose but without the background information, you will have more questions than answers.

So, let's begin…

The human mind is communal by nature. Communion is defined as "being <u>one with</u> someone or something" whereas companionship is defined as "being <u>with</u> someone or something".

In order to maximize the quality of life, every person must seek harmony with the following 4-things.

The Body

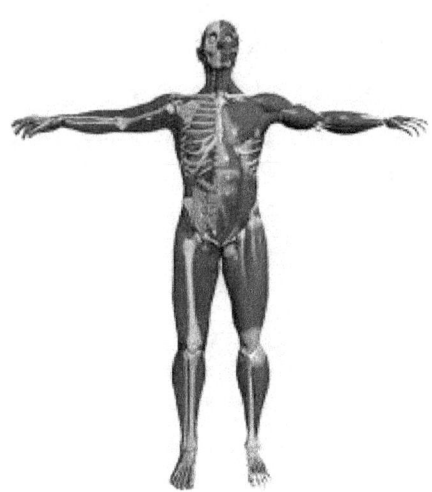

The physical body, of both men and women, is made up of 18 chemical elements, all of which are the exact elements found in soil.

The central nervous system, made up of the brain and spinal cord, controls all the functions of the body.

Two subsystems are employed to assist the central nervous system.

- The somatic nervous system, which controls all skeletal and muscular movements

- The autonomic nervous system, which controls the glands and emotions

In the science of physiology *(the study of the physical body)*, the endocrine system encompasses the glands of the body.

An endocrinologist is a medical doctor, who specializes in this system.

Science tells us that almost all disease originates because of a malfunction in the endocrine system.

It is important to understand that the health of the physical body has a tremendous effect on the mental health of an individual. Not all mental health maladies have mental roots. Many have physical causes and it is important to understand the need for proper nutrition and medical checkups.

Using computer terminology, the autonomic nervous system is the software and controls the brain. Sticking with our analogy, the brain is the computer hardware. The brain, in turn, relies heavily on the information stored on the hard drive, which is the mind. All the parts are connected and the illness of one part affects the health and well being of the other parts.

There exist three important control mechanisms of the body: energy, belief system and the subconscious mind.

Einstein proved (e=mc2) that all matter is controlled by energy, even atoms. All energy has a measurable frequency. In current medical technology, energy frequencies are measured with MRI's, CT scans, PET scans, and EEGs.

It is now possible to use the body's energy to identify and treat unhealthy frequencies. It has been discovered that certain frequencies (about 7.83 hertz) operate in people of remarkable talent: i.e. healers, radionics operators, dousers, shamans, witch doctors, mystics, golden don, priests and priestesses, etc.

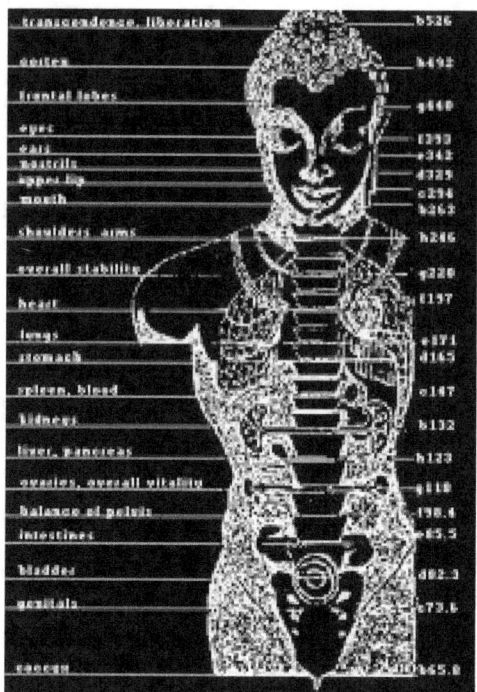

We also know that the optimum human frequency is a little below 7.83 hertz. To drop below this frequency brings on the onslaught of disease.

There are many factors, both internal and external, that affect optimum human frequency. What Einstein may not have realized is that beliefs affect energy.

Research by Bruce Lipton, Ph.D. of Stanford University, shows that biology is controlled by perceptions or beliefs. His work on cells demonstrates how cells are either growing or trying to protect themselves from toxins, or harmful thoughts. Cells in perpetual self-protect mode are more prone to disease, while cells in growth mode are more amenable to wellness.

In human behavior science, we see a similar pattern. Humans are either growing within their minds, or they are attempting to protect themselves from influences and belief systems that bring on anxiety, stress and psychosomatic symptoms.

The subconscious mind, referred to in religious terms as the "heart," is the term we use to describe the control mechanism the body uses to store our beliefs. These beliefs are stored as pictures in our "heart" and create frequencies in our bodies. Harmful beliefs that cause unhealthy frequencies are the source of almost all problems - physical, mental and emotional. If our problems were conscious, we'd have solved them already. Self-help books and many current cognitive therapeutic techniques focus on changing beliefs by painting over existing beliefs with new inputs often with limited success. I have demonstrated previously in one my books, just how easy a painted over belief system can bleed through and manifest itself in previous behavior. Have you ever wondered why?

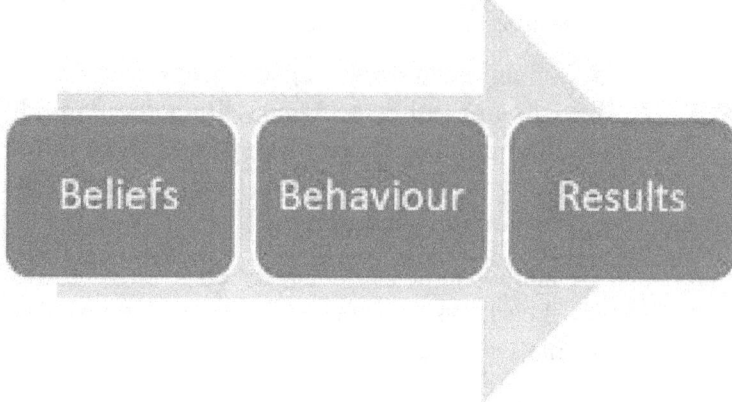

The subconscious mind creates a belief system, which we call "pictures of the heart." These pictures involve either visions or dreams. Dreams are fantasies. Science now tells us the subconscious mind cannot distinguish between fantasy and reality. This is why you cry at sad movies. Your conscious mind knows you are in a theater watching a movie. Your subconscious mind does not.

The subject of all dreams is the dreamer. Dreams are born in our desires, emotions and our will. People who are dreamers tend to gravitate toward the desires, emotions and the will of their psyches, and they believe in a belief system, which is fantasy. A life lived within a fantasy creates a feeling of self-centeredness, hopelessness and despair.

Visions, on the other hand, are pictures of the future that have already been experienced in the heart of those who give it birth. Visions are born in the intellect. Visionary people tend to gravitate toward their intellects. The subject of a vision is not the visionary but the world. Visionaries sacrifice themselves for the good of mankind.

Visions are much more powerful than dreams. Visions have a moral quality that transcends the self-centered nature of dreams. By its very nature a vision launches a mission, a "cause-that-inspires." Visions create a sense of belonging.

Dreams are fantasies that vanish, more often than not, when we wake up. Visions live and grow until their birth. Visions provide the energy of their own fulfillment because visions are born of the spirit. They pulsate with a passion that carries the person who carries them. Visions require no evidence, brush aside all obstacles, and simply ignore the rebukes of those who can't see them. Visions restrain people; dreams and fantasy do the exact opposite and are born of the soul.

We act upon visions and/or dreams using thought. Intellectual thought relies on wisdom; emotional thought relies on the pursuit of pleasure, comfort and delight.

Thoughts evoke action. We act out our thoughts in the form of behavior, and/or conduct. Dreamers live within a facade; they create a false sense of worth using imaginary situations.

Visionaries live within reality; they create change within a framework of restraint and intellectual thought.

Love is born in the intellect while lust is born in the desires, emotions and will. Love is a vision; lust is a fantasy. Love restrains; lust is selfish.

Love is a sense of being one with someone; lust is a sense of being with someone.

Love is communion; lust is companionship. Visionaries love; dreamers lust!

Relationships founded on lust never endure. Lust must be renewed. Once it is not, the two parts attempting to make up one whole tend to be abrasive to one another. Relationships founded on love tend to last.

Love grows and the two parts into one whole, spend a lifetime discovering the mysteries of their mates. Let's go on...

When you break down the human anatomy into its most basic components (subatomic structures), there is absolutely nothing that you can see or touch! Science has proven that the atom, the once assumed basic building block of all matter, is 99.99% EMPTY SPACE! All that exists is energy -- electrical impulses, flowing streams of quantum data, and various frequencies that hold together the small volume of subatomic particles, you call your body.

This energy base enables the chemical reactions, essential to life, to take place, which allows your system to function normally -- digest food, eliminate waste, filter toxins, and so on.

But several factors contribute to the interruption of this energy flow in the body, which results in slow and devastating degradation of the human machine. These include air pollution, chlorine-treated water, pesticides on food, synthetic additives and chemicals put into health supplements.

When these factors disrupt the electrical interaction of your body, it can, and will, manifest as hundreds of symptoms including Heart Disease, Diabetes, Cancer, Fibromyalgia, Allergies, Arthritis, Osteoporosis, Irritable Bowel Syndrome, Chronic Fatigue Syndrome, etc., etc., etc.

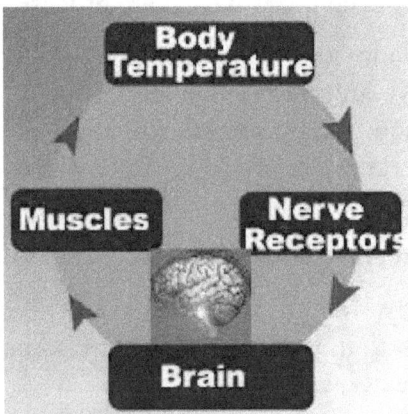

The human body is finely designed to stay in balance (homeostasis) in terms of tissue building up (called anabolism), and tissue breaking down (called catabolism).

An excess of one over the other, is called a metabolic imbalance.

Toxaemia (the buildup of toxins in the body), first occurs as a process of metabolism. Old cells are constantly being replaced by new cells.

In fact three hundred billion or more old cells are called toxic, and must be removed, as soon as possible, by the immune system, through one of four channels of elimination: bowels, bladder, lungs, and skin...and sometimes hurling (lol).

The problem of Toxaemia first occurs when your body is not eliminating toxics at the same rate the toxics are being reproduced.

The second way Toxaemia occurs is from the by-products of foods that are not properly digested.

The major portions of the foods we eat are processed.

Because most of our food has been altered from its original state and we are not biologically adapted to deal with this altered food, the by-products of the incomplete digestion form a certain amount of residue, which builds up in the body.

This residue is also called Toxic.

Regarding your body weight, common sense will tell you that if more of this toxic weight is built up, rather than eliminated, then obesity will occur.

An excess of body fat holds the toxic wastes and attempts to keep the toxins away from the organs of the body.

Toxins are acidic by nature, hence the body retains water to dilute and neutralize the acids in the toxins, adding even more weight and bloatedness.

If the problem goes unchecked, the ultimate result is not only obesity, but also general discomfort, lethargy and a DISRUPTION OF THE ENERGY FLOW OF THE BODY!

In fact, a good deal of the body's finite energy supply is used to eliminate the toxins in the body.

Cleansing of the system frees up energy.

The following problems occur directly because of Toxaemia:

- Cellulite
- irritable bowel syndrome
- arthritis
- swollen ankles/joints
- bad breath
- slow metabolism (increase in weight)
- ulcers
- digestive problems
- migraines
- bad skin
- weak hair and nails
- low immune system
- and kidney problems.

In short, if you disrupt the energy flow of the body, you have big problems, Bubba!

The Mind

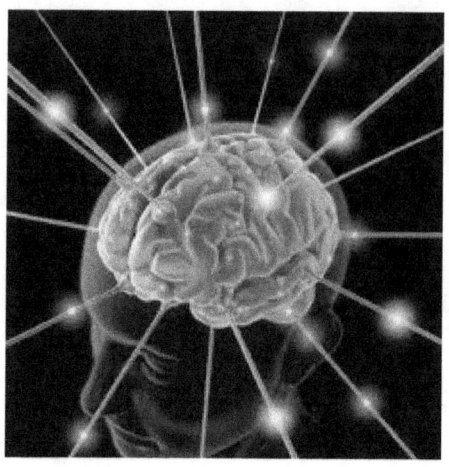

The brain houses the mind, but it is important to understand that the brain is not the mind. The brain is the physical organ where the mind resides. The mind is best described as the intangible interactions within the brain.

I want you to become comfortable with the concept of energy, for I will speak volumes on this subject. Energy, within the body, is basically chemical energy, which produces electricity, and these chemical reactions control the body.

The mind has two parts. One is the conscious mind, which "sees" and evaluates all real stimuli that is received from the five senses (or the ports of the computer).

The second part is the subconscious mind, which "perceives" what the conscious mind "sees". Perception can be very different than reality. This is one of the underlying problems in mental health.

Remember this very important fact: <u>If there is a conflict between the conscious mind and the subconscious mind, the subconscious mind always wins!</u>

Within the subconscious mind lies intellect, this is made up of both empirical, as well as experiential parts. The subconscious mind also contains the desires, emotions and the will of both men and women. The human mind of both genders gravitates towards the desires, emotions, and the will, rather than the intellect. We will discuss this trait in detail.

The mind employs a belief system, which evokes thought. This thought process relies heavily on the intellect, as well as the desires, emotions and will. Thought evokes action. This action is displayed as behavior and/or conduct.

What I have just described is the basic functioning system of the mind, or as we call it in science, "placebo." From this basic system, many things affect placebo and skew the result. As I have already said, culture is not the only factor which skews the mind, but also the male or female orientation received in childhood. This skewing has a tremendous effect on how the psyche is employed, and we will also discuss this in detail.

I spoke earlier about the pictures of the heart. These pictures are your belief system. We animate these pictures into either fantasies, or visions. After the thought process I described above, we express these fantasies or visions through action, which in turn is called behavior and conduct. Another such action is words!

Except for love, the power of words inspired by a vision or fantasy is the most potent human force. Visions evoke strength while fantasies evoke power.

Regarding visionaries- strong people do not generate strong words; strong words create strong people.

Regarding dreamers- powerful people generate powerful words; powerful words do not create powerful people!

To a visionary, strength is made perfect in weakness. To a dreamer, power is made perfect in strength. Words are a form of action, which takes their expression in both our behavior, and/or conduct. Powerful words work either for the good, or bad, or for everyone who uses them with conviction. Conviction comes from embracing a vision or fantasy.

People who choose to speak using profanity constantly amuse me. When I ask why they do this, the typical response is, "They are only words. What harm does it cause?" Interesting statement, eh?

Words are powerful because they define the person speaking them. Words are the result of their underlying belief system. Social mores are still against profanity, but this form of expression is more and more commonly used, and as society comes to accept this expression, social mores are being changed. Cohabitation, drugs and casual sex are just a few examples of how social mores have changed within my lifetime.

A vision provides its own words, words that guarantee its birth. These words will always be simple, distinct, and focused. Dreamers plagiarize their words from imaginary life situations. The strongest words of a visionary touch deeply felt needs. The powerful words of a dreamer touch selfish wants and desires.

The sole purpose of strong words is to transfer the vision from our hearts to the hearts of a needy world. Visionaries do not try to convince, manipulate, or change anyone's mind. A visionary's mission is to communicate the vision in words that instantly create appealing images which harmonize and provide a solution to meet our needs. Visionaries change existing belief systems; dreamers simply pander to them.

Conversely, the sole purpose of powerful words is to transfer the fantasy from our hearts to the hearts of an insecure and lustful world. Dreamers do try to convince, manipulate and change a person's mind. A dreamer's mission is to communicate the fantasy using words that instantly create appealing images that pander to the lusts, desires, comfort and pleasure of those people who embrace a lustful lifestyle.

If you have vision and the words that express it, you will have all the strength to succeed you will ever need.

Everything else is commentary. The meanings of words are not in the words. They are in us.

Living a life in the soul causes us to concentrate on pleasure, selfishness, and material things. These things are the very things we fantasize about. We create whole worlds in our minds, and then choose to walk up and down in our fantasy, neglecting our good. Where is our good? Human activity is often undertaken out of the conviction that <u>our good is somewhere other than where we are</u>. The three kids thought that by getting Tim's blocks, they would also get Tim's fun. They were wrong, and so are you when you undertake to find your value and worth in any other place than yourself.

teenager
(noun)

When you're too young
for half the things you
want to do and too old to
do the other half.

Meanings lie in the feelings, not in the words. Left brain, intellectual logic and content focused words, can be totally accurate and completely wrong! Words that ring and words that sing are words that reach the heart. Weak and predictable words can never penetrate the, "I'm not listening barrier," that guards the heart. Only words that create "instant pictures" have power. When we choose words we have to ask what images they create. How do these word-pictures make the person, I'm addressing, feel?

The mind works by the ear! Words create pictures and pictures talk back. The inner dialogue is called thinking. Sub-conscience thinking is the combining of sounds and preconceived images. How a person perceives this unconscious dialogue determines "conscious decisions." Words that sound good go-to-work <u>immediately</u>! Getting someone's attention requires you to capture the imagination with a picture that is more appealing than the one his or her heart is already watching. The right words are how you do it. Revolutions create the vocabularies that drive them! Everyone who uses the words becomes a teacher.

We also have what I call positioning. Positioning is the battle for your mind to either embrace a vision, or a dream. Positioning is not what you do with the vision or dream; it's what you do in the heart. The easiest way to own the position in the heart is to be first!

When I teach human behavior to salespeople, I teach them that in consumer marketing, the leading brand in any category is almost always, the first brand that has been heard. Whoever owns the position in the heart owns the category!

If you can't be first in your category, create a new category. Marketing is a battle over impressions, not products. Perception is everything!!! When you promote the category, you have no competition.

The most powerful marketing concept is to own a word in a person's heart. Words that "sound good" create positive mental images below conscious thought. Words that sound good together are powerful memory devices.

In life, the leading brand in any category is almost always the first brand that panders to the lusts of a person. As in marketing, whatever owns the first position in the heart owns the category! The category I am speaking about in life is the MIND! If vision is not first in your category, then fantasy becomes first. Life is a battle over perceptions, not impressions. Once again, perception is everything. Everyone perceives FIRST to be best. Whatever you promote in the category you have no competition. If the category (mind), embraces a vision, then it is expressed first. If the category embraces fantasy, then it is expressed first.

A branding iron to the rump will work for cows. Nothing external will brand the human heart. Branding is about how our 10,000 billion brain synapses cause us to feel about a vision or a dream, and by our inherent human natures we always gravitate toward the emotional side of our psyches unless trained to do otherwise.

Branding is the instantaneous evaluation and verdict of every experience, good, or bad that we have had with an emotional trigger. It's an immediate, "thumbs up or thumbs down." Branding is not what we consciously think and determine. It's about what our hearts decide automatically and instantaneously when we hear or see the trigger.

If we don't feel anything, our hearts say, in effect, "return to sender." We constantly want to feel and emote, these feelings. This is the inherent problem between love and lust. Love is born in the intellect and seeks communion. Lust is born in the emotions and seeks companionship. If our human nature is to feel, we naturally gravitate toward lust. Love requires commitment; lust does not. In communion, your wants and needs are last. In lust they are first. Remember one of the paradoxes I taught you earlier- to become first, you must be last. Love is what you should seek!

Effective branding requires making compelling connections to deeply rooted human emotions or profound cultural forces. "Me first!" This is every child's favorite phrase which identifies the most basic human emotion as the need for security. Love is that security, and lust is its counterfeit.

Joy is only possible where people are secure. Power is never created. It is always transferred. When relationships built on lust are mistakenly given the power of the heart, the individual has lost the power to tell the difference. Everyone has a deep desire to create a relationship of value, a longing to belong to someone

23

who loves him or her. Most people never discover a true love relationship. No one has ever received love by practicing lust! You can only receive love when you first give love.

The Soul

In science, we define the soul as the blood and breath of the body. It is important to note that both blood and breath are physical properties; it is the spirit, which is the non-physical property.

Man was designed to live by the spirit, but the soul has usurped the spirit's position, and we now live by the soul instead of the spirit. This is very important. We were designed by our Creator to live within the energy of the spirit, which is infinite. In other words, our spirits were meant to commune with God as one, connected to an infinite source of energy and strength. As I described above, the energy of the body is finite, and it is stored as body fat, or as glycogen in the liver.

Science understands energy very well. There is only one element in the universe that is both matter and energy.

We call this LIGHT! Einstein proved that energy is neither created, nor destroyed.

When we physically die, our bodies are decomposed and returned to the eighteen base elements of the soil. The energy the body held, upon death, is used to decompose the body. In other words, there is a finite amount of matter in the universe, but an infinite amount of energy.

When we live by the soul, we live within a finite paradigm of both matter and energy. When this energy runs out, we die.

Death is described as the soul leaving the body. This "soul" is the breath departing, and the blood ceasing its life- giving properties.

However, our spirits are eternal so let's discuss this for a moment. The soul and spirit are communal in nature, or together as one.

They are distinct and separate entities, but they were designed to be as one, the immaterial parts of our bodies.

This is an important fact. Upon death, our physical body decomposes and returns to the soil, but our soul and spirit live on.

They cannot be separated, but one can usurp the other's divine position of animating the body.

People do not appear to see the difference between the matter part of an organism (the body), and the life part, which animates it (the soul). They seem to think that the organism, itself, is life. We all seem to suffer a similar problem of understanding.

To put it in perspective, in human behavior science, people do not appear to see the difference between their outward habits (conduct & behavior), and the inward part that animates them (belief systems). \

It is not their outward appearance that defines our habits, but their inward experiences and anxieties, and this is where their habits are born. In other words, life is not your physical body. Life is what animates the body.

It is not your conduct, or behavior, which defines who you are, but your inward belief systems. It is your inward belief systems that animate your conduct and behavior.

It is important to always think of both the soul and spirit in terms of energy. When you do this, the soul represents finite energy; the spirit represents infinite energy.

The Spirit

In my definition of the mind, I have referred to the energy of the body. The mind utilizes energy, made within the body, in the form of chemical reactions. The spirit is that very energy that the mind uses. If you believe my premise that man was designed to live by the spirit, then the mind was actually designed to be a subsystem of the spirit.

Wisdom resides in the intellect, and we were designed to employ our intellects first, and then decide if a situation requires an emotional response.

This is homeostasis. We now live by the soul; the soul requires the pursuit of comfort, pleasure and self-gratification, which is no different from other animals on the planet. Sound familiar?

Because we now live by the soul, it is our inherent nature to gravitate toward our desires, emotions, and will instead of our intellects. Here is where our problems begin.

If we had continued to live by the spirit, we would have employed our intellects first, as a given inherent virtue, powered by an infinite source of energy, but because we live by the soul, we gravitate to our desires, emotions and will; using a finite amount of energy, in the form of stored energy, body fat, and manufactured energy, using the chemical reactions of the body.

Let's see if I can pull all of this together for you.

Remember I said that both blood and breath are physical properties, and that it is the spirit which is the non-physical property.

As physical animating properties, it is the soul that serves our physical bodies. The body craves comfort, pleasure and gratification.

If our spirits were the animating force of the body, we would enjoy the fruits of the spirit, which are love, joy, peace, long-suffering, gentleness, goodness, faith, meekness, and temperance (self-control).

The spirit does not serve the body only; it serves the mind and soul, too. In other words, it serves the complete person. Conversely, the soul only serves the body.

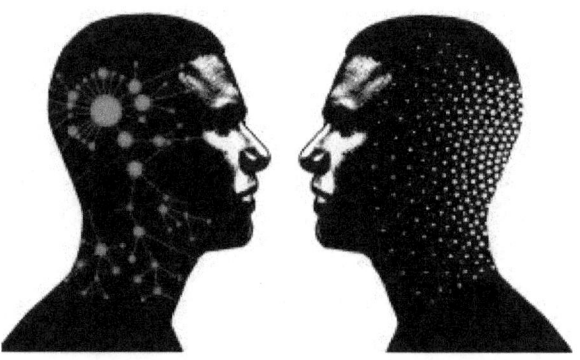

Men evaluate everything subconsciously based upon how much energy will be required to accomplish a given task.

Women do not do this. However, science tells us that women have upwards of 50% more body fat than men. Interesting, eh?

If you believe my premise that man was originally designed to live by the spirit, then it easy to see what my conclusions are here.

To live by the spirit is to live within an infinite amount of energy that is never depleted.

Since the soul is a part of the spirit, the animating force of the body would be linked to an infinite source of energy. Hence, there would be no death.

When mankind switched to living by the soul instead of the spirit, man began to gravitate toward his/her desire, emotions and will, instead of employing his/her intellect.

It is in the intellect that the spirit resides. With that said, and as I previously alluded to, if we were originally designed to live by the spirit, then we were originally designed to live hooked to an infinite amount of energy.

There would be no death, and this is exactly what occurred prior to the fall of Adam and Eve in the Garden of Eden.

But, by living by the soul, we live within a finite framework of energy, and when it is depleted, we die.

The body renews the depletion of energy by nutrition; however, when sickness occurs, and the energy expended is greater than the energy renewed by our diets, we die.

Chapter 1 – Changes

Change is not an inherent trait in humans. We are in love with the status quo even if it is harmful. The reason behind this trait is that we fear the unknown. We will talk about fear later on in the book. We would rather have something that is known rather than unknown.

In order to better understand what I will be presenting in this chapter I need to teach you what is called "The Mechanism of the Mind," which the mind uses to achieve behavior/conduct/action.

The Mechanism of the Mind

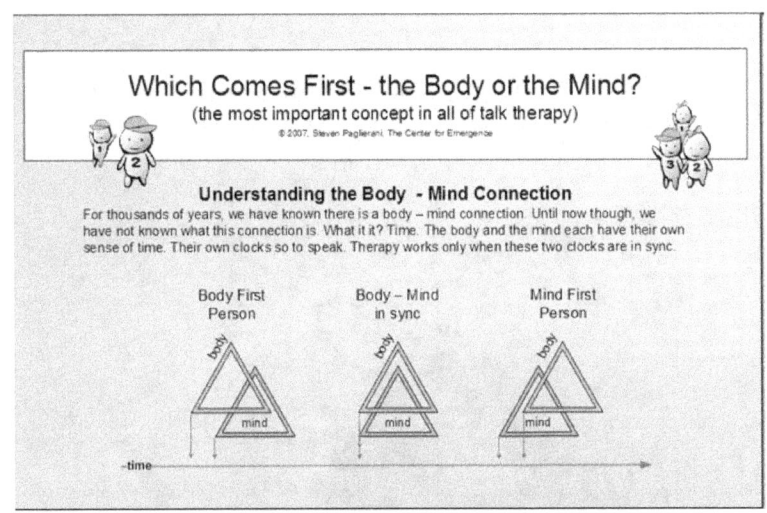

Which Comes First - the Body or the Mind?

(the most important concept in all of talk therapy)

© 2007, Steven Paglierani, The Center for Emergence

Understanding the Body - Mind Connection

For thousands of years, we have known there is a body – mind connection. Until now though, we have not known what this connection is. What it it? Time. The body and the mind each have their own sense of time. Their own clocks so to speak. Therapy works only when these two clocks are in sync.

Body First Person

Body – Mind in sync

Mind First Person

time

Prior to the fall of man into sin as described in the Garden of Eden, man's spirit was hooked to God's infinite spirit. There was no death because God's spirit is infinite. Man is the only animal on earth that shares the eternality nature of God.

The subject of eternal life has been a heated topic of man from the beginning of our existence.

In Greek mythology, there's a story about a mortal youth named Tithonus. Aurora, the goddess of dawn, fell in love with the boy and when Zeus, the king of the gods, promised to grant Aurora any gift she chose for her lover, she asked that Tithonus might live forever.

But, in her haste she forgot to ask for eternal youth, so when Zeus granted her request, Tithonus was doomed to an eternity of perpetual aging as a grouchy old man… forever.

In the movie "Highlander," Angus McLeod was born in 1518 as an immortal being. He could not die and to me, the best part of the movie was the depiction of this immortal's agony here on earth as he watched everything he loved die forcing him to begin his life over and over again. He saw all of the ugliness, which man had caused over four centuries. He witnessed the Spanish Inquisition, Waterloo, the atrocities of the Third Reich, and more. He saw the slavery and bigotry of the eighteenth century, the slaughter of the Native American tribes after the Civil War. This man's life was a living Hell!

There is a very big difference between the ways our feeble minds picture eternal life versus God's idea of eternal life. Our understanding comes from Quantum Physics and is limited within the Time-Space Continuum.

Life is your spirit, but the soul of man has usurped the spirit's position and psychology is now forced to define "how" we live our lives based on the animating force of the soul instead of the spirit. As I said previously, the soul has usurped the spirit's place as our animating force. Let's discuss this now.

- ❖ **Body First Person** - When the body becomes our life, we live as animals.
- ❖ **Body-Mind In Sync** - When the soul becomes our life, we live as rebels and fugitives in a life of desires, emotions, and will (consuming entities). This is the position of mankind today!
- ❖ **Mind First Person** - But when we come to live our life in the mind/spirit and by the spirit, though we still use our soul's faculties just as we do our physical faculties, they are now the servants of the spirit.

If you live as a consuming entity, you will always lose. In other words, to get, you must give - you must sacrifice! Have you ever wondered why you have so many anxieties, phobias, worries and fears? You do not give; you take and hold on to things when you should let go! The reality of this world is evil.

So what is reality? I will tell you. This is reality:

"Life without war is impossible either in nature or in grace. The basis of physical, mental, moral and spiritual life is antagonism. Health is the balance between physical life and external nature, and it is maintained only by sufficient vitality on the inside against things on the outside.

33

Everything outside my physical life is designed to put me to death. Things, which keep me going when I am alive, disintegrate me when I am dead. If I have enough fighting power, I produce the balance of health.

The same is true of mental life. If I want to maintain a vigorous mental life, I have to fight, and in that way the mental balance called thought is produced. Morally it is the same.

Everything that does not partake of the nature of virtue is the enemy of virtue in me, and it depends on what moral caliber I have whether I overcome and produce virtue (GOOD CHARACTER).

Immediately I fight, I am moral in that particular. No man is virtuous because he cannot help it; virtue (character) is acquired.

- ❖ Psychology only studies the observable aspects of the mind and discounts the unseen or intangible aspects of the human mind.
- ❖ Behavioral science attempts to study the intangible aspects of the human mind…why you do the things you do and more importantly why you don't do what you should do.
- ❖ There is no such thing as commercial psychology versus personal psychology. The mind uses the same mechanism to evaluate all types of relationships.
- ❖ Everything we do revolves around relationships. We relate to our environment, our friends, family, co-

workers, other people and even our pets.　We are
social animals.

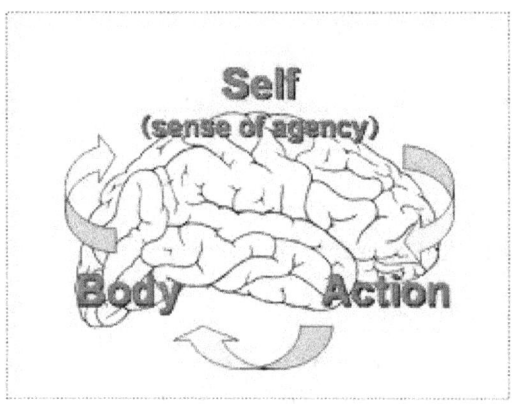

The Actual Mechanism of the Mind

**Belief Systems + Thought + Delight =
Action/Behavior/Conduct**

**Your Conscious Mind "sees" reality for what it is and
reacts…**
5-senses:
Sight
Hearing
Taste
Touch
Smell
ESP (women only)

**Your Subconscious Mind "perceives" reality and
interacts…**
Intellect:
Experiential

35

Empirical

DEW:
Desires, Emotions and Will

The Human Psyche Differences Between Genders

The female psyche operates on emotional, spiritual, physical and intellectual planes
The male psyche operates only on the intellectual and physical planes.

Here is an exercise you might find weird but it demonstrates the power of the human mind.

Fi yuo cna raed tihs, yuo hvae a sgtrane mnid too. Cna yuo raed tihs? Olny 55 plepoe out of 100 can. I cdnuolt blveiee taht I cluod aulaclty uesdnatnrd waht I was rdanieg. The phaonmneal pweor of the hmuan mnid, aoccdrnig to a rscheearch at Cmabrigde Uinervtisy, it dseno't mtaetr in waht oerdr the ltteres in a wrod are, the olny iproamtnt tihng is taht the frsit and lsat ltteer be in the rghit pclae. The rset can be a taotl mses and you can sitll raed it whotuit a pboerlm. Tihs is bcuseae the huamn mnid deos not raed ervey lteter by istlef, but the wrod as a wlohe. Azanmig huh? Yaeh and I awlyas tghuhot slpeling was ipmorantt!

You might have found it somewhat unusual that you could probably read the jumbled mess above.

Actually over half the people that see this exercise can decipher the words at the same speed of reading as if the words were not jumbled.

It is important to note that the human mind thinks in packages…concepts rather than individual ideas.

Your eyes see each letter but the mind looks at the whole word instead. As you read, the mind looks at the first and last letter only.

If you were to listen to an orchestra, your ear listens to every note from every instrument but a trained ear can actually pick out individual instruments from the whole sound as the mind hears the whole symphony.

How does this apply to you?

Learning to observe means going beyond the mind's natural ability to only read the first and last letters of a word.

It is training the mind to see all the letters, not just the eye but the mind! The freedom of letting go begins with retraining the mind.

Truisms About the Human Mind

- ❖ Pain vs. Pleasure – people are more motivated to avoid pain than seek pleasure.
- ❖ A person that is suffering depression will seek relief (notice I didn't say cure) before they seek happiness.
- ❖ The human mind cannot tell the difference between fantasy and reality.
- ❖ The human mind gravitates to the desires, emotions and will of its psyche. People grave entertainment so fantasy dominates their existences.
- ❖ The human mind is easily distracted! You can either be the cause of these distractions or other stimuli will be the cause but rest assured people WILL BE distracted because the human mind is gullible.

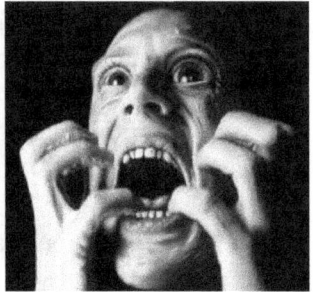

The human mind responds quickly to these three forms of stimuli

- ❖ Sex
- ❖ Humor
- ❖ FEAR

But the greatest of them all is FEAR! We will discuss fear in a later chapter.

BTW – on the positive side we have faith, hope, love, but the greatest of these is LOVE.

Fear usually takes the form of what is called "Scarcity Thought"

You are afraid that someone will have what you feel belongs to you or that others will have more "stuff" than you.

- ❖ The subconscious mind is often referred to as the "heart," and is the control mechanism the body uses to store our beliefs.

❖ **These beliefs are stored as pictures in our "hearts" and create frequencies in our bodies.**

❖ We know that the optimum human frequency is a little below 7.83 hertz. To drop below this frequency brings on the onslaught of disease. To rise above it a person demonstrates psychic abilities.

❖ Harmful beliefs that cause unhealthy frequencies are the source of almost all problems - physical, mental, emotional.

❖ The subconscious mind creates a belief system, which we call "pictures of the heart."

❖ These pictures involve either visions, or dreams/fantasies.

❖ Science has discovered that the subconscious mind cannot distinguish between fantasy and reality.

*The subject of all dreams is the dreamer.
*Dreams are born in our desires, emotions and will.
*Dreamers believe in a belief system, which is fantasy.
*A life lived within a fantasy creates a feeling of self-centeredness, hopelessness and despair.   In dreams everything is perfect.

IMPORTANT: The main problem of letting go is that a person fantasizes the situation into something it is not and lives within the fantasy rather than the reality.   If there is a conflict between the conscious mind and the subconscious mind then the subconscious mind ALWAYS wins...ALWAYS!

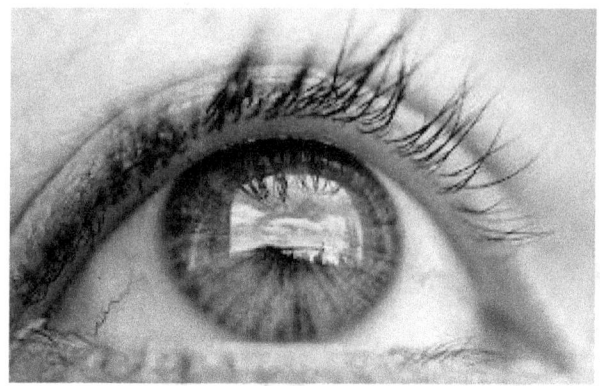

*The subject of a vision is not the visionary but the world.

*Visions are born in the intellect.

*Visions are pictures of the future that have already been experienced in the heart of those who give it birth.

*Visionaries sacrifice themselves for the good of mankind.

*Visions have a moral quality that transcends the self-centered nature of dreams.

*By its very nature a vision launches a mission, a "cause-that-inspires."

*Visions create a sense of belonging.

❖ We act upon visions and/or dreams, using thought.

❖ Thought employs the intellect, in the case of visions, or the desires, emotions and the will, in the case of dreams.

❖ Intellectual thought relies on wisdom; emotional thought relies on the pursuit of pleasure, comfort and delight.

❖ Dreamers live within a facade; they create a false sense of worth using imaginary situations.

- ❖ Visionaries live within reality; they create change, within a framework of restraint, and intellectual thought.
- ❖ The world is made up of OPPOSITES, which is usually the corrupted version of the original. We have good and evil. We have love and lust!
- ❖ EVERYTHING YOU DO IS BECAUSE OF LOVE OR LUST. Learn to love because there are no crimes beyond forgiveness.

*Love is born in the intellect; lust is born in the DEW!
*Love is vision; lust is fantasy.
*Love restrains & sacrifices; lust is selfish
*Love is being one with someone or something
*Lust is being with someone or something.
*Visionaries love; dreamers lust!
*Visionaries do what is required; dreamers just do their best!

WHEN THERE IS NO HOPE OF LOVE DO WE ABANDON OURSELVES TO LUST?

Yes we do!

Pictures of the heart are your belief system.

- ❖ We animate these pictures into either fantasies, or visions.
- ❖ People do not appear to see the difference between the matter part of an organism and the life part, which animates it.

43

- ❖ We seem to think that the organism itself is life. In other words, it is not our outward appearance that is our life, but our inward existence.
- ❖ Life is what goes into the body. Death is what comes out.
- ❖ A person who lies is not a liar because he tells a lie. The lie is the manifested behavior of some subconscious belief system. The lie only demonstrates that the person is a liar…it is the effect.
- ❖ Except for love, the power of words inspired by a vision or fantasy is the most potent human force.

"Do you want to have or do you want to be?"

*For a dreamer: "Seeing is believing!"
*But they only see imaginary things that are not real!!

*This is why "The Secret" is WRONG!

*Say it and claim it is WRONG!

*Blab it and grab it IS WRONG!

*See it and be it IS WRONG!

Dreamers practice companionship – To be with someone or something!

VERY IMPORTANT:

1. Dreamers covet the object of their temptation, BUT they covet the temptation more so than the object itself because the temptation is the idol of their fantasy.
2. If there is a conflict between the conscious and subconscious mind, the subconscious mind always wins...ALWAYS!
3. All reaction occurs in the conscious mind; all interaction occurs in the subconscious mind. Fear is a "REACTION" to losing control.

For a visionary: "Believing is seeing!"

There are no SECRETS; there are only challenges to be conquered!

THIS IS NOT A SECRET: Putting a photo of a Ferrari on your refrigerator and seeing yourself driving it by employing the so-called law of attraction is pure BUPKES!!! Why? Because this is all occurring in the conscious mind and beliefs reside in the subconscious mind.

How do you transfer something from the conscious mind to the subconscious mind and make it a belief system?

A Ferrari is the object of your temptation but what you covet most is the temptation of owning a Ferrari because the temptation is the idol of your fantasy. It is all about ATTENTION & ACCEPTANCE!!!!!

I have a $100 bill in my hand and I am willing to give it to you. But if you don't ACCEPT it then it is still in my hand. BELIEF SYSTEMS ARE CREATED BY ATTENTION & ACCEPTANCE!

John 1:12 But as many as received him, to them gave he **the right** to become children of God, even to them that believe on his name

Human things must be known to be loved; but divine things must be loved to be known.

BELIEVING IS SEEING!

*****

Okay, change is difficult because it requires us to step away from our fantasy and the human mind never gives up anything that is sensuous. This is why sexual addiction is almost impossible to cure.

Changing your fantasy requires changing your belief system and later on I will discuss this in detail.

For now, let's discuss the issue of control...

Chapter 2 - Control

Control is a subject near and dear to most people. Fear is a conscious mind reaction to being out of control. It is a reflex rather than a behavioral trait.

Once the reaction takes place, your belief systems embedded in your subconscious mind takes over and all of your actions/behavior/conduct result from your subconscious mind!

In other words, your conscious mind has nothing to do with letting go of anything. It only sees reality. Your subconscious mind is responsible for letting go and this is where the battle resides.

To demonstrate, let's talk about goals for a minute…

Goals

Which of the following goals are good goals?

❖ To want to get married and have a wonderful, happy, loving marriage?
❖ To want to have children who are happy, successful, and loving?
❖ To have a successful, fulfilling and rewarding career?
❖ Is it a good goal to want to have fun, bonded, loving, and meaningful relationships with other people?

Which of the listed goals are good goals? None of them!

You should never have anything for a goal that is not 100% under your control, AND each and every goal should be <u>motivated by love</u>. You are only in control of YOURSELF; not your kids, not your spouse, not your friends and acquaintances and definitely NOT your relationships!!!

Almost all goals that we have in our life are wrong. Everything that we do, we do because of a goal we have. When we get up in the morning, it's because of some goal that we have; we are hungry for breakfast, or we need to go to work. If we go to the grocery store, it's because of some goal we have. If we are kind to people, it's because of some goal that we have.

Now we don't always know what they are, because a lot of these are subconscious goals. The goals we have are the reasons for everything we do. But, do all of your goals involve only YOU?

Of course not!

And when the other person, or persons, in your goal do not perform, or act the way you want them to, then we become anxious and stressed.   When our goals get blocked, it creates anger, anxiety, and frustration. If we only have good goals, we will not experience anger or anxiety.   That's how you know, if you are living a wrongful goal. If the result is anger and frustration because your control was blocked and blocking your goal, then you had a wrongful goal.

It may have been a fine and noble desire, but a wrongful goal. It is important to note with what I have revealed above is that your belief systems and subsequent thought patterns determine all of your actions and conduct, without exception.

In letting go, it is necessary to realign your belief systems and thoughts to a more correct mindset and begin to see the change in you.

Chapter 3 - Fear

We have touched on the subject of fear a little bit previously. Now I want to discuss it in detail since this is one of the three main things that affect our well-being.

Here is an article by Karl Albrecht that I think you will find interesting:

http://www.psychologytoday.com/blog/brainsnacks/2012 03/the-only-five-basic-fears-we-all-live

Fear is a vital response to physical and emotional danger—if we didn't feel it, we couldn't protect ourselves from legitimate threats. But often we fear situations that are far from life-or-death, and thus hang back for no good reason. Traumas or bad experiences can trigger a fear response within us that is hard to quell. Yet exposing ourselves to our personal demons is the best way to move past them.

President Franklin Roosevelt famously asserted, "The only thing we have to fear, is fear itself." I think he was right, actually.

Fear of fear probably causes more problems in our lives than fear. That claim needs a bit of explaining, I know.

Fear seems to have gotten a bad rap amongst most human beings. And it's not nearly as complicated as we try to make it.

A simple and useful definition of fear is: An anxious feeling, caused by our anticipation of some imagined event or experience.

Medical experts tell us that the anxious feeling we get when we're afraid is a standardized biological reaction. It's pretty much the same set of body signals, whether we're afraid of getting bitten by a dog, getting turned down for a date, or getting our taxes audited.

Fear, like all other emotions, is basically information. It offers us knowledge and understanding - if we choose to accept it - of our psychobiological status.

There are only five basic fears, out of which almost all of our other so-called fears are manufactured. Those five basic fears are:
Extinction - fear of annihilation, of ceasing to exist. This is a more fundamental way to express it than just calling it the "fear of death". The idea of no longer being arouses a primary existential anxiety in all normal humans.

Consider that panicky feeling you get when you look over the edge of a high building.

Mutilation - fear of losing any part of our precious bodily structure; the thought of having our body's boundaries invaded, or of losing the integrity of any organ, body part, or natural function. For example, anxiety about animals, such as bugs, spiders, snakes, and other creepy things arises from fear of mutilation.

Loss of Autonomy - fear of being immobilized, paralyzed, restricted, enveloped, overwhelmed, entrapped, imprisoned, smothered, or controlled by circumstances. In a physical form, it's sometimes known as claustrophobia, but it also extends to social interactions and relationships.

Separation - fear of abandonment, rejection, and loss of connectedness - of becoming a non-person - not wanted, respected, or valued by anyone else. The "silent treatment," when imposed by a group, can have a devastating psychological effect on the targeted person.

Ego-death - fear of humiliation, shame, or any other mechanism of profound self-disapproval that threatens the loss of integrity of the Self; fear of the shattering or disintegration of one's constructed sense of lovability, capability, and worthiness.

That's all - just those five.

Think about the various common labels we put on our fears. Start with the easy ones: fear of heights or falling is basically fear of extinction (possibly accompanied by significant mutilation, but that's sort of secondary). Fear of failure? Read it as fear of ego-death. Fear of rejection? It's fear of separation, and probably also fear of ego-death. The terror many people have at the idea of having to speak in public is basically fear of ego-death. Fear of intimacy or "fear of commitment" is basically fear of losing one's autonomy.

Some other emotions we know by various popular names are also expressions of these primary fears. If you track them down to their most basic levels, the basic fears show through.

Jealousy, for example, is an expression of the fear of separation, or devaluation: "She'll value him more than she values me." At the extreme, it can express the fear of ego-death: "I'll be a worthless person." Envy works the same way.

Shame and guilt express the fear - or the actual condition - of separation and even ego-death. The same is true for embarrassment and humiliation.

Fear is often the base emotion on which anger floats. Oppressed peoples rage against their oppressors because they fear - or actually experience - loss of autonomy and even ego-death. The destruction of a culture or a religion by an invading occupier may be experienced as a kind of collective ego-death. Those who make us fearful will also make us angry.

Religious bigotry and intolerance may express the fear of ego-death on a cosmic level, and can even extend to existential anxiety. "If my god isn't the right god, or the best god, then I'll be stuck without a god. Without god on my side, I'll be at the mercy of the impersonal forces of the environment. My ticket could be canceled at any moment, without a reason."

Some of our fears, of course, have basic survival value. Others, however, are learned reflexes that can be weakened or re-learned.

That strange idea of "fearing our fears" can become less strange when we realize that many of our avoidance reactions - turning down an invitation to a party if we tend to be uncomfortable in groups; putting off the doctor's appointment; or not asking for the raise - are instant reflexes that are reactions to the memories of fear.

They happen so quickly that we don't actually experience the full effect of the fear. We experience a "micro-fear" - a reaction that's a kind of shorthand code for the real fear. This reflex reaction has the same effect of causing us to evade and avoid as the real fear. This is why it's fairly accurate to say that many of our so-called fear reactions are actually the fears of fears.

When we let go of our notion of fear as the welling up of evil forces within us - the Freudian motif - and begin to see fear and its companion emotions as basically information, we can think about them consciously. And the more clearly and calmly we can articulate the origins of the fear, the less our fears frighten us and control us.

Or, maybe not...

Chapter 4 – Hooked on a Feeling

Good name for a song, eh?

What does "hooked on a feeling" have to do with letting go? Here is a fantastic article from ABC News that says it better than me.

Hooked on a Feeling: The Dangers of Behavioral Addictions

By LISA MILLER
Women's Health
Oct. 13, 2012

http://abcnews.go.com/Health/WomensHealth/hooked-feeling-dangers-behavioral-addictions/story?id=17463393#.UONZDlv39Bk

Anne* was 34 years old when she thought she'd found her soul mate. Never mind that she was already married with three kids at home.

This new guy -- actually, her former high school English teacher -- made her laugh; he exhilarated her; he got her. A schoolteacher herself, Anne started skipping out of work early to meet him. "It was incredible, exciting, and miserable all at once," she says. Just like falling in love.

Except this wasn't quite love!

Fueled by a soon-insatiable hunger for the high that comes with a new romance, Anne began jumping from affair to affair. Yahoo! Personals was, literally, her gateway to satisfaction in her small, conservative Arkansas town. She had standards, of course: Her boyfriends, as she thought of them, couldn't be married (even though she was), and she responded only to suitors who were highly educated (she was a teacher, after all). Eventually, she was sneaking out while her husband slept. She bought secret cell phones and hid them all over the house, in her car, under her bra.

"It got crazier and crazier," she says. "I needed more and more."

The urgency was, she guessed, similar to what crystal-meth addicts must feel. She wasn't far off. The driving forces behind compulsions like Anne's are surprisingly similar to, and can be just as detrimental as, what makes an alcoholic crave booze or a drug addict jones for a score. But whereas drinks or pills are easily measurable, behaviors are not. And thanks to a culture obsessed with obsessions, behavioral dependencies--to things such as gambling, stealing, shopping, exercise, sex, and, yes, love -- can balloon from common indiscretions into destructive threats before women realize they're in trouble.

Downplaying the Detriment

Anne's story may seem sensational, but cases like hers are increasingly documented, and countless people are now addicted to compulsive behaviors. So prevalent is gambling addiction, for instance, that it is included in the psychiatric bible, the Diagnostic and Statistical Manual of Mental Disorders, or DSM. (Substance addictions are a big problem as well: More than 23 million Americans are addicted to drugs or alcohol, according to the Substance Abuse and Mental Health Services Administration, and more people than ever are hooked on prescription painkillers.)

Sneakier than their substance counterparts, behavioral addictions--sometimes called process addictions at treatment centers--are difficult to measure and present a boatload of diagnostic challenges. For years, addiction doctors wouldn't acknowledge them as legitimate--after all, who doesn't love food or sex? A woman who works out every day could be mentally ill or enviably fit; Anne's love addiction stemmed from a serious compulsion, yet wives who cheat on their husbands aren't always addicts. The now-accepted difference between a habit and a dependency lies in this definition of addiction: Continued compulsive use of a mind-altering substance or behavior

60

with negative life consequences. In English: If your behavior harms you or others and you still can't stop, you could be dealing with a serious sickness.

The problem is, it's hard to reflect on whether your tendencies are dangerous when everybody everywhere seems to be addicted to something--or at least that's what they say. "I'm so addicted to these cookies," friends confide to each other, or these jeans, these spinning classes, that dating show. Search the hashtag #addict on Twitter and discover a world of habits and cravings, real and exaggerated: People confess addictions to shoes, diet soda, Forever 21, nail biting, and (naturally) Twitter.

Even life-altering dependencies are now regarded in a more casual way. In the cultural ground zero of Hollywood, for example, addictions, once shameful and scandalous, are almost completely out of the closet. Celebs speak openly about needing rehab, and their relapses somehow seem less shocking. With addiction so glamorized and addiction-talk so common, it can be hard for many addicts to see their problem as a problem . . . before it's far-gone.

Behavioral addiction plays a big part in a person's need to hang on and not let go. But all addiction comes from fantasy and not intellect.

Anne, in the above story was not weary of suffering under her addiction; Anne was weary of pleasure and this is the most profound definition of addiction.

But here's the catch; the article states the following:

A woman who works out every day could be mentally ill or enviably fit; Anne's love addiction stemmed from a serious compulsion, yet wives who cheat on their husbands aren't always addicts. The now-accepted difference between a habit and a dependency lies in this definition of addiction: Continued compulsive use of a mind-altering substance or behavior with negative life consequences. In English: If your behavior harms you or others and you still can't stop, you could be dealing with a serious sickness.

There is a big distinction between addiction and habit. I address this in my book, "You Can't or You Won't

You "can't" because you are an addict; you won't because it is a habit. Get It?

Chapter 5 – Allowing Things to Control You

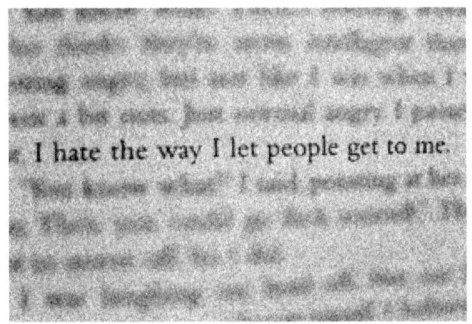

Let's go back to Chapter 2 and the subject of control. Addiction aside, let's talk about habits.

One of my associates – Charles Duhigg – wrote the following article and is one of the leading authorities on habit formation.

http://www.npr.org/2012/03/05/147192599/habits-how-they-form-and-how-to-break-them

Habits: How They Form And How To Break Them

Routines are made up of a three-part "habit loop": a cue, a behavior and a reward. Understanding and interrupting that loop is key to breaking a habit, says journalist Charles Duhigg.

Think about something it took you a really long time to learn, like how to parallel park. At first, parallel parking was difficult and you had to devote a lot of mental energy to it. But after you grew comfortable with parallel

parking, it became much easier — almost habitual, you could say.

Parallel parking, gambling, exercising, brushing your teeth and every other habit-forming activity all follow the same behavioral and neurological patterns, says New York Times business writer Charles Duhigg. His new book The Power of Habit explores the science behind why we do what we do — and how companies are now working to use our habit formations to sell and market products to us.

How Habits Form

It turns out that every habit starts with a psychological pattern called a "habit loop," which is a three-part process. First, there's a cue, or trigger, that tells your brain to go into automatic mode and let a behavior unfold.

"Then there's the routine, which is the behavior itself," Duhigg tells Fresh Air's Terry Gross. "That's what we think about when we think about habits."

The third step, he says, is the reward: something that your brain likes that helps it remember the "habit loop" in the future.

Neuroscientists have traced our habit-making behaviors to a part of the brain called the basal ganglia, which also plays a key role in the development of emotions, memories and pattern recognition. Decisions, meanwhile, are made in a different part of the brain called the prefrontal cortex. But as soon as a behavior becomes automatic, the decision-making part of your brain goes into a sleep mode of sorts.

"In fact, the brain starts working less and less," says Duhigg. "The brain can almost completely shut down. ... And this is a real advantage, because it means you have all of this mental activity you can devote to something else."

That's why it's easy — while driving or parallel parking, let's say — to completely focus on something else: like the radio, or a conversation you're having.

"You can do these complex behaviors without being mentally aware of it at all," he says. "And that's because of the capacity of our basal ganglia: to take a behavior and turn it into an automatic routine."

Studies have shown that people will perform automated behaviors — like pulling out of a driveway or brushing teeth — the same way every single time, if they're in the same environment. But if they take a vacation, it's likely that the behavior will change.

"You'll put your shoes on in a different order without paying any attention to it," he says, "because once the cues change, patterns are broken up."

That's one of the reasons why taking a vacation is so relaxing: It helps break certain habits.

"It's also a great reason why changing a habit on a vacation is one of the proven most-successful ways to do it," he says. "If you want to quit smoking, you should stop smoking while you're on a vacation — because all your old cues and all your old rewards aren't there anymore. So you have this ability to form a new pattern and hopefully be able to carry it over into your life."

Marketing Habits

It's not just individual habits that become automated. Duhigg says there are studies that show organizational habits form among workers working for the same company. And companies themselves exploit habit cues and rewards to try to sway customers, particularly if customers themselves can't articulate what pleasurable experience they derive from a habit.

"Companies are very, very good — better than consumers themselves — at knowing what consumers are actually craving," says Duhigg.

As an example, he points to Febreeze, a Proctor & Gamble fabric odor eliminator that initially failed when it got to the market.

"They thought that consumers would use it because they were craving getting rid of bad scents," he says. "And it was a total flop. People who had 12 cats and their homes smelled terrible? They wouldn't use Febreeze."

That's when Proctor & Gamble reformulated Febreeze to include different scents.

"As soon as they did that, people started using it at the end of their cleaning habits to make things smell as nice as they looked," he says. "And what they figured out is that people crave a nice smell when everything looks pretty. Now, no consumer would have said that. ... But companies can figure this out, and that's how they can make products work."

Companies can also figure out how to get consumers to change their own habits and form new ones associated with their products or stores. The megastore Target, for example, tries to target pregnant women, says Duhigg, in order to capture their buying habits for the next few years.

"The biggest moment of flexibility in our shopping habits is when we have a child." Charles Duhigg

"The biggest moment of flexibility in our shopping habits is when we have a child," he says, "because all of your old routines go out the window, and suddenly a marketer can come in and sell you new things."

Analysts at Target collect "terabytes of information" on its shoppers. They have figured out that women who buy certain products — vitamins, unscented lotions, washcloths — might be pregnant and then can use that information to jump-start their marketing campaign.

This can get tricky: One father was upset after receiving coupons for baby products in the mail from Target addressed to his teenage daughter.

"He went in and said, 'My daughter is 16 years old. Are you trying to encourage her to get pregnant?' and the manager apologizes," Duhigg says. "The manager calls a couple of days later...and the father says, 'I need to apologize...I had a conversation with my daughter, and it turns out there's some things going on in my house that I wasn't aware of. She's due in August.' So Target figured it out before her dad did."

Okay, habit formation is a powerful force in human beings because we package things in our minds so as to not forget them.

Back when I was at UCLA in my undergraduate program, I remember an event that has always fascinated me.

I remember watching TV and an interview came on with a Vietnam POW. The intervicwer asked the man how he survived the torture, the pain and depression of imprisonment. The man's answer literally stunned me. He replied, "I learned to love it!"

Can you believe it? The man literally trained himself to become a masochist. Now that he was home and back amongst the people he loved, he commented that untraining himself was more difficult.

So, the million dollar question is "How do we get rid of bad habits?" or "untrain" ourselves? One of my associates – Scott Young wrote a very good article on this very subject...you do it not by "untraining" yourself but by replacing the bad habit with a good one.

18 Tricks to Make New Habits Stick

By Scott H Young

Wouldn't it be nice to have everything run on autopilot? Chores, exercise, eating healthy and getting your work done just happening automatically. Unless they manage to invent robot servants, all your work isn't going to disappear overnight. But if you program behaviors as new habits you can take out the struggle.

With a small amount of initial discipline, you can create a new habit that requires little effort to maintain. Here are some tips for creating new habits and making them stick:

*1. **Commit to Thirty Days** – Three to four weeks is all the time you need to make a habit automatic. If you can make it through the initial conditioning phase, it becomes much easier to sustain. A month is a good block of time to commit to a change since it easily fits in your calendar.*

*2. **Make it Daily** – Consistency is critical if you want to make a habit stick. If you want to start exercising, go to the gym every day for your first thirty days. Going a couple times a week will make it harder to form the habit. Activities you do once every few days are trickier to lock in as habits.*

*3. **Start Simple** – Don't try to completely change your life in one day. It is easy to get over-motivated and take on too much. If you wanted to study two hours a day, first make the habit to go for thirty minutes and build on that.*

*4. **Remind Yourself** – Around two weeks into your commitment it can be easy to forget. Place reminders to execute your habit each day or you might miss a few days. If you miss time it defeats the purpose of setting a habit to begin with.*

*5. **Stay Consistent** – The more consistent your habit the easier it will be to stick. If you want to start exercising, try going at the same time, to the same place for your thirty days. When cues like time of day, place and circumstances are the same in each case it is easier to stick.*

*6. **Get a Buddy** – Find someone who will go along with you and keep you motivated if you feel like quitting.*

*7. **Form a Trigger** – A trigger is a ritual you use right before executing your habit. If you wanted to wake up earlier, this could mean waking up in exactly the same way each morning. If you wanted to quit smoking you could practice snapping your fingers each time you felt the urge to pick up a cigarette.*

*8. **Replace Lost Needs** - If you are giving up something in your habit, make sure you are adequately replacing any needs you've lost. If watching television gave you a way to relax, you could take up meditation or reading as a way to replace that same need.*

*9. **Be Imperfect** – Don't expect all your attempts to change habits to be successful immediately. It took me four independent tries before I started exercising regularly. Now I love it. Try your best, but expect a few bumps along the way.*

*10. **Use "But"** – A prominent habit changing therapist once told me this great technique for changing bad thought patterns. When you start to think negative thoughts, use the word "but" to interrupt it. "I'm no good at this, but, if I work at it I might get better later."*

*11. **Remove Temptation** - Restructure your environment so it won't tempt you in the first thirty days. Remove junk food from your house, cancel your cable subscription, throw out the cigarettes so you won't need to struggle with willpower later.*

*12. **Associate With Role Models** - Spend more time with people who model the habits you want to mirror. A recent study found that having an obese friend indicated you were more likely to become fat. You become what you spend time around.*

*13. **Run it as an Experiment** - Withhold judgment until after a month has past and use it as an experiment in behavior. Experiments can't fail; they just have different results so it will give you a different perspective on changing your habit.*

*14. **Swish** - A technique from NLP. Visualize yourself performing the bad habit. Next visualize yourself pushing* *aside the bad habit and performing an alternative. Finally, end that sequence with an image of yourself in a highly positive state. See yourself picking up the cigarette, see yourself putting it down and snapping your fingers, finally visualize yourself running and breathing free. Do it a few times until you automatically go through the pattern before executing the old habit.*

*15. **Write it Down** – A piece of paper with a resolution on it isn't that important. Writing that resolution is. Writing makes your ideas more clear and focuses you on your end result.*

*16. **Know the Benefits** - Familiarize yourself with the benefits of making a change. Get books that show the benefits of regular exercise. Notice any changes in energy levels after you take on a new diet. Imagine getting better grades after improving your study habits.*

*17. **Know the Pain** – You should also be aware of the consequences. Exposing yourself to realistic information about the downsides of not making a change will give you added motivation.*

*18. **Do it For Yourself** - Don't worry about all the things you "should" have as habits. Instead tool your habits towards your goals and the things that motivate you. Weak guilt and empty resolutions aren't enough.*

Chapter 6 – Letting Go of Love

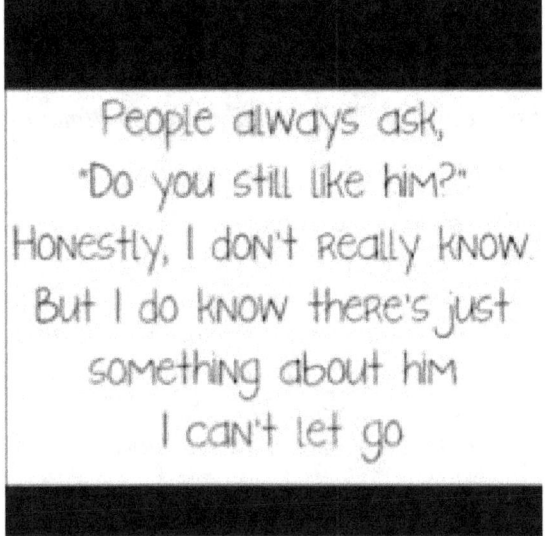

Letting go of love is a very formidable task. We all desire to be admired and loved. But like I said previously, we have all loved and lost.

Below is an article b y Dr. Phil that really nails the topic.

Letting Go of Love
By Dr. Phil

http://www.drphil.com/articles/article/172

Have you been dumped, betrayed or left so heartbroken that you didn't ever want to love again? Are you still stuck on an ex and don't know how to move on? And how do you know when it's time to let go and look for love somewhere else?

● *If you're "the other woman" who's waiting for a man to leave his lover, don't waste your time. "If he'll do it with you, he'll do it to you," Dr. Phil says. The man you want lacks integrity and can't make a commitment.*

● *Are your standards too low? Dr. Phil asks a guest who's waiting around for a man that's let her down time and again: "What is it about you that causes you to settle for somebody that you know will cheat on you, know will lie to you, know will make a commitment and then break it? What is it about you that you believe about yourself that you're willing to settle for that?" Recognize that you're settling and that you deserve more. Set a higher standard for yourself.*

● *Does he really even make you happy? Be honest with yourself about the extent to which he's really meeting your needs. Chances are you're longing for the relationship that you wish it could be, and that you want to be in love with the person you wish he was. Dr. Phil reminds a guest: "There are times when you break up with somebody and you start missing them and you start thinking about all the good things. And then you're back with them for about 10 minutes and you go 'Oh yeah! Now I remember why I hate you!'" Don't kid yourself about what it was really like or glorify the past.*

● *Don't wait around because you think he's going to change. The best predictor of future behavior is past behavior, so the chance that he's going to ride in on his*

74

white horse and do the right thing is pretty slim. Dr. Phil explains, "To the extent that there's some history, you don't have to speculate, you just have to measure."

Don't put your life on hold. Every minute you spend focusing on your ex is a minute that's holding you back from a better future. Dr. Phil tells his guest, "As long you are obsessed on this guy, you will never put your heart, soul and mind into getting your life in order and starting another relationship if you want one." Set some goals and start putting your life back together.

Ask yourself: Are you hiding in the relationship so you don't have to face the reality of being on your own? Don't stay with someone because it's comfortable and safe. It may seem more secure, but it's not healthy for you and it certainly won't help you get to a better place. Why would you want to settle and waste your life away just to avoid getting back in the game?

Be clear with him. "You've got to say not just 'no,' but 'hell no,'" Dr. Phil tells his guest. "'Get out of my life. Stay away from me. Don't call me.'" If you live together, it's time to move out, or you may need to change your phone number. Dr. Phil reiterates: "Do what you have to do." If the circumstances are more complicated or severe, you may need to get a lawyer in order to get child support or to hold him accountable for any other outstanding issues.

Don't hold all men responsible for the mistake your ex made. Why should he pay for the sins of someone else who may have wronged you?

Learn to trust again — by trusting yourself. Dr. Phil tells a man who's having a hard time letting women back into his life: "Trust is not about how much you trust one person or another to do right or wrong. How much you trust another person is a function of how much you trust yourself to be strong enough to deal with their imperfections." Have enough faith in yourself to be able to put yourself on the line with someone, without any guarantee of what will happen next. If you're playing the game with sweaty palms, it's because you're afraid of what you can or can't do, or dealing with your own imperfections — it's not about the other person.

Know that you will get hurt if you're in a relationship. There is no perfect person without flaws. Even a well-intended guy is going to hurt his partner. He's going to hurt your feelings. He's going to say things that you don't want him to say. He's going to do things you wish he wouldn't do and not do things you wish he would do. A relationship is an imperfect union between two willing spirits who say, "I'd rather be in a relationship and share my life, share my joys, share my fun, share my activities, share my life than do it alone." If you want to be in a relationship, know that getting hurt comes with the territory. You just have to decide that you are durable enough, that you have enough confidence in yourself that you can handle it.

Don't invest more than you can afford to lose. While it's important to move forward, you need to take things one step at a time. Don't put so much out there that you'll be emotionally bankrupt if things go south.

76

Don't beat yourself up. You got through your last experience, you've learned from it, and now it's time to move forward. Dr. Phil tells his guest, "You'll move on and be a champion in your next endeavor as you did in your past ... Life is not a success-only journey. You are going to get beat up along the way."

Focus on yourself. All of us come into relationships with baggage, but you need to have closure on past experiences before you can start a new relationship with the odds in your favor. Dr. Phil tells a guest who's had trouble with her father, her brother and two previous husbands: "Unless and until you've figured out everything you've got to figure out about that and you get closure, you will never come into a relationship with a fresh and clean heart and mind and expectancy and attitude." You're probably not ready to get into another relationship until you heal the wounds of your past.

Listen to what he's saying. If he's telling you that you want different things out of life and there's no way you can work as a couple, don't turn his words around into what you want to hear. He's being quite clear.

Know the statistics. Dr. Phil tells a guest who's waiting for her ex to come around: "There's a 50/50 chance a marriage is going to work if both people are head over heels in love, passionate and willing to climb the mountain, swim the river and slay the dragon to get to each other. That's with everybody crazy in love and running toward each other in that field that we see in the commercials. The problem you've got here is he's running the other way in the field! So if it's 50/50 when you're running toward each other, what do you think it is when

77

the other person is running out of the field and hiding in the woods?"

Being alone makes some people actually break out in hives.

They prefer a bad relationship to no relationship at all.

In numerous counseling sessions, I have discovered that people will go to any and all lengths to avoid being alone and some of these "lengths' are pretty weird.

In one such case I even wrote a complete book on this lady I refer to in my book, "Too Late For Fruit; Too Soon For Flowers"

But living alone is not as bad as one thinks. I address this subject in detail in my book "Living Alone"

Living Alone

Loneliness is not being without someone.
Loneliness is being without love!

Dr. Harry Jay

The thought of living alone requires change and we have already discovered that change isn't something most people relish.

Chapter 7 – This Is Your World; Shape it or Someone Else Will

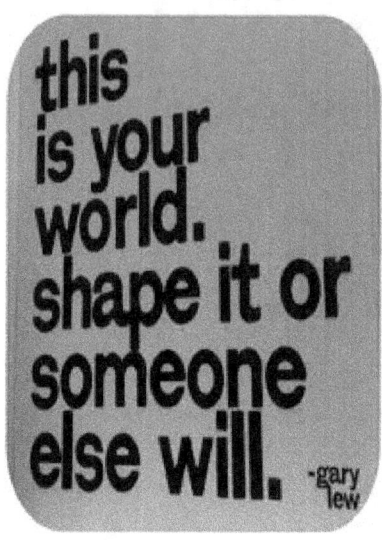

Acceptance in the Human Mind

Is the human mind free to accept or reject any belief system?

I believe that the answer to this question goes right to the heart of the difference between science and religion. By restricting yourself to seeing the world through a filter of objective (observer independent) observation, you basically force the world to fit into the activity of "the observer studying that which is apart from himself." This is unavoidable because if the observer interacts with what he observes then the nature and character of the observer becomes relevant in what is observed and that means it is no longer observer independent. It means that the observation procedure will obtain different results depending on who does it, and when that happens science does not recognize any evidence upon which it can draw conclusions.

This does not mean that science does not recognize these limitations, or even that it does not draw conclusions from it. Quantum physics is certainly one of the most familiar examples to me. It recognizes that the act of measurement not only alters what is being measured but also tends to create the very thing being measured. Examples of how science has to navigate around this limitation in many fields of science shows just how unavoidably real it is. And I think this is how a scientist can perceive a serious flaw in the naturalist presumption that what science describes is all that is real. Certainly psychologists have come to realize how belief affects perception, and this is one of the things that show just how important this objectifying technique of science can be in understanding the world, for it allows us to go beyond the limitations of our belief to discover things about the world that we could never have imagined. Modern medical science has to constantly confront and navigate around the placebo effect by using control groups in the test of a possible cure for disease.

Thus there is absolutely no denying that belief effects what we observe - it is scientific fact. My question is not whether belief affects reality, but how?

Simple logic suggests that what this limitation of the methodology of science is going to affect most is when the subject of our observation is closer to the observer himself. So it is no accident that I use two examples – science and religion. But what I want to do is to look at the serious flaw involved in trying to force self-examination to fit into the scientific activity of the observer studying that which is apart from himself. The apparent contradiction is quite obvious. But just try to imagine what this says about some of the typical situations in life where we are forced to examine ourselves. For example, consider the question of love. Do you love this person? The question is not avoidable because it involves some rather important decisions about how you will live your life? But can you answer such a question by examining yourself as if you were a bug under a microscope. When people do try this, they usually fail. It is a scenario examined by quite a number of books and films. The critical element that this approach usually misses is the answer to the question - do you want to love this person?

There is dissonance between answering such a question and the usual standard of scientific objectification, where what you observe should not depend on what you want.

To avoid misunderstanding, let me make a clarification about what topic I am addressing. If we consider the question, "Does the belief about a particular thing have an effect on the reality of that particular thing?" It should be clear that the answer in general is "no." This is not true for all things because we must distinguish those things that we have no control over from those which are very much subject to our own decisions.

Now I am not saying that everything can be neatly categorized in one or the other, our health is one of the things where the two intimately interact. Even within the question of health, the distinction is there. The body requires the function of the heart and kidneys in order to continue living. If these fail and are not replaced then you will die, and wanting it to be otherwise will not change this.

On the other hand, doctors see all the time how the desire to live plays a critical role in whether their patients survive. The reason I believe that all this ties into the nature of religion is because religion imposes upon our perception of reality, beliefs about the way things should be.

Religion constantly confronts us with the question, "what kind of person we want to be?" It studies the question of how our choices and our beliefs affect the living of our lives - not only the choices of an individual but also in society. Thus I believe that within religion, in addition to its arbitrary cultural baggage, there is a reservoir of experience about the answers to such questions. It is frustration about the difficulty in distinguishing between these two that often causes people to abandon it altogether.

The point here is that for all science is useful and truthful. It is not the "be all and end all" of human life. It is not simply enough to understand the world around us. We have to decide what to do with that understanding. We have to decide how we are going to live our lives.

And that is not something that science can answer because it is not simply a question of what is, but also a question of what we want to be.

We are not just observers looking at life as if it were something apart from ourselves. We are participants, and what we decide to do (and to believe) has an enormous impact on the kind of life we are going to experience.

Indeed there are some new age religions which have tried to throw out all the cultural and doctrinal baggage in order to focus on the role of religion exclusively (such as the Church of Religious Science). One thing that should be clear is that not everyone is going to answer the question in the same way, and the result is that diversity in the area of religion is just going to be a reality that we have to accept and one that I hope we can learn to embrace.

What is the purpose of the human brain?

What function does it serve? Be careful. This is a trick question! If you say "the brain is an organ of thought" or "the brain is an instrument of knowledge" or "the brain is the way we understand the world," that's the wrong answer. The correct answer is that the brain is an organ of survival. We have these big brains because they enabled our ancestors to survive. In that sense, they are no different from claws or fur or fangs. And like all organs of survival, the brain was shaped by natural adaptations that favored the traits that helped our ancestors survive. The big brains we have now were initially molded and shaped for one purpose- to help small bands of hunter-gatherers survive.

Back in the day, when we rarely lived longer than 20 or 25 years and starvation battled with predation by large predators for the top spot in the list of "things that killed human beings," our brains gave us a competitive advantage. They did this in part by acting as engines of belief, allowing us to form models of the world and create beliefs about the world that gave us an edge.

For example, an early human who observed that if he was upwind from his prey, the prey got away, but if he was downwind from his prey, he could more easily kill it formed a belief: "Staying downwind from the prey makes it more likely that the prey will not escape."

Of course, other animals know these things instinctively. But the advantage of our big brains is that we do not have to rely on instinct; we can form beliefs on the fly, as we go along, which means we can function in environments our instincts are not prepared to deal with.

The brain as an organ of survival allows us to make observations and draw beliefs from these observations, and these beliefs give us a competitive advantage.

These beliefs can be immediate and concrete, such as "If I stick my hand in the fire, it will hurt." They can make predictions about the future, such as "The sun will rise tomorrow" or "If the days grow longer and the weather grows colder, then winter is coming, and food is about to become less plentiful." A belief can be negative, such as

"If I leap from the top of this tree, I will not be able to fly." Having a brain optimized for forming beliefs is important if forming beliefs is your survival strategy. If you think of the brain as a belief engine, which can either believe something or disbelieve it, and if you think of a particular belief as being true or false, it is easy to construct a game theory matrix describing all the possibilities, with two success modes and two failure modes:

Ideally, our brains lead us to believe things that are true, such as "A large leopard is a dangerous adversary," and to disbelieve things that are not true, such as "I can eat rocks." But there are two failure conditions as well: rejecting beliefs that are true and accepting beliefs that are not.

The failure conditions have survival implications. Believing untrue things and not believing true things can both lead to disaster. Of the two, though, believing things will, in a small group of hunter-gatherers, usually cause fewer problems than not believing things. Believing that dancing in circles three times and carrying a magic stone around with you will increase the chances of a successful hunt doesn't really hurt anything; not believing that staying downwind from your prey is important has a significant survival penalty attached to it. There's a strong survival imperative, in other words, to prefer failure by believing something untrue over failure by not believing something that is true.

Believing is less expensive than not believing.

If a primitive hunter-gatherer eats an unfamiliar food and then becomes sick, it might not be the food that caused him to get sick--but if he believes the food makes him sick, and he's wrong, the consequences are not too great. Whereas if he does not believe the food made him sick, and he's wrong, the consequences can be deadly. The guy who ate some food, got sick, and believed the food made him sick is the guy who survived; today, his descendants give their kids a measles vaccination, and when, coincidentally, their kids are diagnosed with autism, they believe that the measles vaccination caused the autism.

From a survival standpoint, the consequences of not believing something true are worse than the consequences of believing something that is not true. Natural adaptation, therefore, tends to select in favor of people whose default state is to believe something rather than in favor of people whose default state is to disbelieve something. And to confound matters further, humans are social animals.

In our earliest days, when our social groups tended to number fifty or a hundred people and leopards were a serious and ongoing threat, to live alone was a death sentence. We depended on the support of others to survive. But that support had a price. Groups, like individuals, form beliefs. To reject the beliefs of your group was to risk ostracism and death.

People who questioned and challenged the beliefs of their tribe often did not survive to pass on their genes to future generations; the ones that were most likely to pass along their genes were the ones who learned to believe what the group believed, even if it was contradicted by clear and available evidence.

And those who were adept at manipulating the belief engines of others--shamans, tribal rulers who convinced others of their divine right to rule--tended to be disproportionately successful at mating and tended to control a disproportionate amount of resources, meaning they tended to pass on their genes most successfully.

The greatest invention of the human mind is not fire, or agriculture, or iron, or the steam engine, or even the splitting of the atom. From the perspective of understanding the physical world, the greatest invention of the human mind is the scientific method--the systematic, skeptical approach to claims about the way the world works.

When a scientist has an idea, he does not believe it, and he does not seek to prove it. Instead, he approaches it skeptically, and he seeks to disprove it.

The more the idea resists increasingly sophisticated and vigorous attempts to disprove it, the more faith he begins to put in it. This is why any idea that is not falsifiable is not science. A corollary of this idea is the notion that physical reality behaves the same way everywhere, for everyone. If a brick falls when it is dropped in Kansas, it also falls when it is dropped in Salt Lake City--and, importantly, it falls no matter who drops it, whether the person who drops it believes that it will fall or not. The physical world does not change itself to conform to human wishes and expectations.

A claim that is made about some process that must be believed in order to be seen, such as ESP, is not science.

But skepticism is not innate; it is learned. The human brain has been shaped by natural adaptation not to be skeptical.

It has been shaped by adaptive pressure into a belief engine that believes things more easily than it disbelieves things.
For our ancestors, the penalty of skepticism was very high; those early hominids for which skepticism came naturally did not live long enough to pass on their genes to us.

Our brains evolved to be gullible, not skeptical.

Today, we live in a cognitive and physical environment very different from our ancestors. But the machinery of natural adaptation is slow. In the modern world, the same four states of our belief engines still apply. We are still predisposed to believe things rather than disbelieve them, and we can still believe things that are true, disbelieve things that are true, believe things that aren't true, or disbelieve things that aren't true:

What does this mean in practical terms? Simple; it means that your brain has been hard-wired over thousands of years of natural adaptation to make you gullible. Look at the brain as an instrument of survival, look at natural adaptation creating pressures to prefer the failure mode of believing that which isn't true over the failure mode of

89

not believing that which is true, and you end up with people hard-wired from the ground up to be credulous and to accept new beliefs without question. Your brain is a tool of survival that works by acting as an engine for creating beliefs. When you form a belief, you get a little squirt of pleasure that light up the reward circuit of your brain. You're emotionally rewarded every time you believe something. At the same time, skepticism and rational, analytical thought do not come naturally. They're not what your brain was optimized for, and because of that, these are skills which must be learned, and are not innate. In fact, they feel unnatural and uncomfortable to you. Your brain gives you a reward for accepting beliefs, not for challenging them.

There is good news, however. When you introduce sapience into the mix, things change. Biology is not destiny. Your brain is optimized to make you gullible, but you do not need to be.

You can train yourself to recognize that little squirt of pleasure you get when you believe something for what it is--a biological holdover from a time when adopting beliefs quickly and without skepticism had survival advantage.

You can train yourself to be skeptical, even though it's not natural for you. And the rewards for doing so are great. In a modern world, where people want you to believe that they will transfer THE SUM OF $250,000,000 (TWO HUNDRED FIFTY MILLION USD) into your bank account from Nigeria if you give them your bank account information, where emails tell you that you need to update your credit card information or PayPal will shut you down, where people tell you that viruses and bacteria don't cause disease and if you just order magic "balancing powder" ($360 for a 6-month supply) from their website you'll never get sick, credulity is a survival disadvantage, and skepticism is an advantage. But it doesn't come naturally. You have to work at it.

Reality, Belief and The Mind

One major problem in the world today (and this applies especially to "educated" people") is that they are not really very smart. Actually "smart" is not the right word. What I am trying to say is that they are not very perceptive and suffer from a marked inability to look and see things as they actually are.

The reason for this is that they are the most familiar with the ideas and notions of the times, having been thoroughly "educated" (a better word is indoctrinated) into these notions and ideas. This "education" (indoctrination) generally acts to create a set of cultural or "professional" blinders (filters) which prevents the "educated" person from viewing or understanding anything outside of the current "professional" framework that they have been indoctrinated into. It's not that they lack and need more knowledge, but that the knowledge that they do have, in and of itself, acts to prevent them from being able to view and understand anything outside their often limited framework of beliefs and attitudes - a framework that they assume to be all-inclusive and often quite perfect.

The rest of the culture goes along with everything that they promote as "facts" and "truth," because these viewpoints and attitudes tend to be everywhere - newspapers, magazines, TV, schools and colleges. In fact they are labeled professionals and command respect irregardless of their character.

One thing is certain…something is going to shape your world and it might as well as be you.

Chapter 8 – How To Let Go

let go.
surrender.
taste freedom.

The Incredible Power of Focus

One of the more important points I have made has been the idea that you really do create your own life and your own reality. I know this idea has become a kind of personal growth cliché that many of us have heard over and over for years. Many people, after continuing to experience the same old ups and downs and personal dramas over many years, get to the point where they dismiss this idea as charming but useless -- or just plain wrong. "If I'm creating this, then I'm certainly not doing it on purpose," they say. "It sure seems like this is HAPPENING to me, rather than that I'm creating it." They just assume that it's all BS because "this and this and this and this are going on for me, and I have no control over it, and anyone who thinks I'm creating this doesn't understand what I'm going through." Essentially, they are resigning themselves to becoming a victim of circumstances.

We live in a universe of infinite complexity and many forces -- way too many to keep track of -- operate on us. Yes, it is true that we are NOT in control of everything that happens, because we are not in control of most of those infinite other parts of the universe. In fact, the only thing you have total and complete control over is...YOUR OWN MIND. That is, if you learn how to exercise it.

Luckily, this one thing -- your mind -- that you do have control over gives you tremendous power. By exercising control over your mind, you can get the rest of those infinite other parts of the universe to begin to march in formation.

The person who says, "If I'm creating this, it certainly isn't on purpose," is right. They are not creating what is happening to them "on purpose." Who would purposely create failure, or bad relationships, or any other kind of suffering? You can only do something that is not good for you; that is harmful to you, if you do it subconsciously. This means if you are creating something you don't want, you must be doing so subconsciously.

Your mind is running on automatic pilot, based on "software" (subconscious programming) installed when you were too young to know any better, by parents, teachers, friends, the media, and other experiences and influences. The key is to become more conscious, more aware...to get yourself off automatic pilot. Once you do this, you stop creating all the dramas and other garbage you don't want in your life.

94

How do you do this? One way is by remembering and using a very important piece of wisdom. What is this important piece of wisdom? I'm glad you asked.

It's the fact that whatever you focus on manifests as reality in your life.

You are always focusing on something, whether you are aware of it or not. If I spent some time with you, and heard your history, I could tell you what you are focusing on. How? By looking at the results you are getting in your life. The results you get are always the result of your focus.

The problem is this focus is usually not conscious focus; it's automatic or subconscious focus. We subconsciously focus on something we don't want, and then when we get it we feel like a victim and don't even stop to think that we created it in the first place. And what is more, we don't realize we could choose to create something completely different if we could only get out of the cycle of subconsciously focusing on something other than what we want.

If you have a significant negative emotional experience (say, for instance, a relationship in which you are abused or mistreated in some way), a part of you is going to say: "Okay, I get it. There are people out there who can and will hurt me. Relationships can be dangerous and painful. I have to watch out for these people [or sometimes, relationships in general] and avoid them." Unfortunately, to watch out for them and avoid them, you have to focus your mind on "people who could hurt me," or "bad relationships," and that focus draws more of what you don't want to you...AND...actually makes these things you don't want (at least initially) attractive to you, so when they appear in your life you are drawn to them. This is why many people keep having one relationship after another with the same person, but in different bodies. This, of course, applies to everything, not just relationships. I'm just using relationships as an example.

Focusing on what you do not want, ironically, makes it happen. Focusing on not being poor makes you poor. Focusing on not making mistakes causes you to make mistakes. Focusing on not having a bad relationship creates bad relationships. Focusing on not being depressed makes you depressed. Focusing on not smoking makes you want to smoke. And so on. I think you get the idea. The mind will create what you focus on both GOOD and BAD!!!

The truth is your mind cannot tell the difference between something you think about or focus on that you DO want, and something you think about or focus on but do NOT want. The mind is a goal-seeking mechanism, and an extremely effective one at that. Already, all the time, it is elegantly and precisely creating exactly what you focus on. You are already a World Champion Expert at creating whatever you focus on. You couldn't get any better at it, and you don't need to get any better at it.

When you focus on anything, your mind says: "Okay, we can do that," and starts figuring out how to do it. It doesn't ask whether you're focusing on it because you want it or because you do not want it. It ALWAYS assumes you want what you focus on and then it goes and makes it happen. The more frequent and the more intense the focus, the faster and more completely you will create what you have focused on, which is why intense negative experiences create intense focus on what you do not want, and tend to make you re-create what you don't want, over and over.

Most of the time, for most people, all the focusing and thinking is going by at warp speed, on automatic, without much, if any, conscious intention. Your job is to learn how to direct this power by consciously directing your focus to the outcomes you want. Once you do, everything changes. This does, however, take some work, because at first you have to swim upstream against the current of your old, unconscious habits, and the current can be swift and strong. Trained observation actually teaches you to focus on what you want.

First, you have to discover all the things you focus on that you do not want, and I'm willing to bet there are quite a few -- way more than you think. To the degree you're getting what you don't want, you are focusing, albeit subconsciously, on what you don't want.

Spend some time over the next few weeks making a list of all the things you do NOT want as you notice yourself thinking about them.

Second, you have to get very clear about what you DO want. Then, you have to examine each of the things you want and be sure they are not just something you do NOT want in disguise. For instance, saying "I want a relationship where I am treated well" would not even be an issue if you had not had relationships where you were not treated well, and even in making this seemingly positive statement you are focusing on not wanting to be mistreated. Saying "I want a reliable car" wouldn't even come up if you weren't focusing on the fact that you don't want a car that breaks down and needs a lot of repairs.

After you've sorted out the things you habitually focus on that you do not want, and know what you do want, you have to begin to notice each time you think about an outcome you do not want, and consciously change your thinking, right in that moment, so you are instead focusing on what you do want.

Remember, you do NOT have to avoid things to be happy and get what you want. The urge to avoid something is a result of having had a negative emotional experience regarding that thing, and trying to avoid things requires you to focus on them, which tells your brain to create them. Not good.

You will be surprised how often you are thinking about what you do not want, how difficult it is to catch yourself doing it every time, and -- most of all – how difficult it is to switch your thinking to what you DO want. There is a strong momentum to keep thinking about that thing you want to avoid. As I said, the current is strong and swift, especially at first.

The solution? Practice, practice, practice! Persistence, persistence, persistence!!!

It's a very good idea to write down what you want, very specifically, so that your Fairy Godmother, were she to read it, would know exactly what to give you without any additional explanation.

Then, read what you have written to yourself, preferably out loud, several times a day, while seeing yourself, in your mind, already having what you want.

Believing is seeing and not the other way around as the world teaches you!

The more emotion you can bring to it, the better. Then, take whatever action is available to begin moving toward what you want. A good time to do this reading and visualizing is when you first wake up and before you go to bed.

I know this is work. Do it anyway. There is a price for everything, and this is the price you must pay to get what you want. Be prepared to pay it. It will be worth it, I promise. And be prepared to pay for a while before you get results. Stick with it.

Another way to change your focus is to ask questions. As an example, I'll ask you one right now. What did you have for breakfast this morning? To answer this question (even to just internally process the question), you had to shift your focus from whatever your mind was focused on (hopefully, to what I am teaching) to today's breakfast.

This means that to change your focus, all you have to do is...ask yourself a question!

It also means you better be careful what questions you ask yourself. Good questions include "How can I get X?" "How can I do X?" "How can I be X?" By asking these kinds of questions, you get your mind to focus on what you want to have, do, or be. Then, your mind takes over and answers the question...solves the problem...and creates what you want. You just have to provide the focus, take whatever action presents itself, and be persistent (some things take time).

I would do away with questions like "What's wrong with me?" or "Why can't I find someone to love me?" and so on. Your mind will find an answer to any question you give it, including these disempowering questions.

Learn to say "How can I...?" when you don't know what to do, instead of "I can't," and (if you are persistent in asking) you will receive the answer, every time. Learn to be conscious in what you focus on and your whole life will change.

This all may seem very utopian to you, or overly simplistic, or like a lot of work. I assure you it is not utopian (it's the way all successful people think), it IS simple, but not simplistic, and yes, it is work, at first. The great Napoleon Hill, who spent over 60 years studying the most effective and most successful people of the 20th century, concluded that -- without exception -- "whatever the mind can conceive and believe, it can achieve." He at first suspected there had to be exceptions, but toward the end of his life he said he had to admit he had not found ANY.

Let's go over that again: "Whatever the mind can conceive and believe it can achieve."

It will take some time to learn how to consciously focus your mind. It will require some effort. You will fail many times, and it will seem difficult. But at a certain point you will "get it" and at that point it will become as automatic as the unconscious focusing you have been doing. When that happens, a whole new universe of power will open to you.

More on Focusing

"And be not conformed to this age, but be transformed by the renewing of your mind, in order to prove by you what is the good and pleasing and perfect will of God."

The one thing in your life you can command is your own mind. Whatever negative people and situations you face, you can always choose a positive attitude. But doing so requires a firm, strong commitment.

Helpful: Begin by writing a self-convincing creed – I believe I can direct and control my emotions, intellect and habits with the intention of developing a positive mental attitude. Post it where you'll see it when you get up in the morning. Read it during the day, and say it aloud. Speaking an intention reinforces it. Choose a "self-motivator" – a meaningful phrase tailored to help you reach your positive thinking goals. Examples:

❖ Counter discouragement with the phrase "Every problem contains the seed of its own solution."

101

❖ Fight procrastination with "Do it now."

Keep your self-motivators nearby – in your pocket or on your desk – and repeat them throughout the day to instill these important new values.

Develop A Life Plan. Setting short and long-term goals each day creates a road map for your life. But only set GOOG goals!!! What is a good goal? One where you are 100% in control and one that is founded in love! A goal of raising good, healthy and prosperous children is a bad goal because you are not in control of what your kids choose. See the important difference? The goal is noble but it is not a good goal.

You identify where you're going, focus your mind on getting there and avoid many wrong turns.

Helpful: Use the D-E-S-I-R-E formula as a goal-setting guideline...

❖ **D**etermine what you want. Be exact, and express the goal positively. Say what you want to be or do rather than what you don't want.
❖ **E**valuate what you'll give in return. How much work will you do to turn your plan into action?
❖ **S**et a date for your goal. Be realistic, allowing enough time without postponing it too long.
❖ **I**dentify a step by step plan. Devise immediate, small steps to get started.
❖ **R**epeat your plan in writing.

❖ Each and every day, morning and evening, read your plan aloud as you picture yourself already having achieved your goals.

Writing out your daily goals helps maintain your motivation. Keep them in your pocket or purse to read frequently throughout the day.

The Power of Visualization

Because visual images reach into our deepest mental levels, I have found pictures to be profound motivational tools. Why? Remember the mind holds everything as pictures!

Helpful: Make a list of personal qualities you want to develop…write down the names of people with whom you would like to have better relationships. Now clip pictures from magazines and newspapers that symbolize your goals.

Example: If generosity is your chosen quality, you could use a photo of someone with an outstretched hand.

Put the pictures where you'll see them everyday…and believe that you will get what you have visualized. You may also create your own "mental pictures" to defeat negative thoughts, such as dwelling on past reversals.

Maintain A Positive Focus. Giving yourself positive experiences actually reinforces your positive attitude.

Examples…

❖ Treat your five senses every day. Listen to your favorite music, taste a food you love, enjoy a beautiful view, etc.

❖ Cultivate a sense of humor. Laughter relaxes tension, and seeing the funny side of things helps you take yourself less seriously.

❖ Smile when you feel like frowning. Smile at yourself in the mirror. If this makes you laugh at yourself, the smile will be that much more real.

Now realize the optimistic face you show the world creates positive thoughts about you in everyone you meet.

How to Train Your Subconscious Mind

Did you know that often the difference between success and failure is the ability to train your mind to focus on achieving your goals and not focus on problems? It's been proven by researchers and by some of the most successful people in the world.

Getting your mind to focus and concentrate on success - so that it finds solutions instead of focusing on the problems is usually the difference between success and failure. But how do you do this?

I'm about to show you how. I'll outline the importance of training your mind, how to start directing your subconscious mind, and how to keep your mind focused so that you constantly achieve your goals and live the life you want. Disciplining your mind so that it is focused on your goals is crucial to your success. If your mind is not trained to focus on and achieve your goals then you really have little chance of success. Your conscious mind is a direct link to your subconscious mind.

So if your mind is focused on your goals and is trained to achieve those goals then your subconscious mind will also be focused on those goals and will attract the situations and opportunities for you to achieve the success you want. It's really that simple.

The minute you get distracted for a prolonged period - you lose sight of your objective and fail to accomplish those goals. In order for to enjoy success - the mind has to be regularly focused on your goals - you can't stay focused for short bursts and expect to get results.

Think of it this way, your riding in a car driven by your personal driver and every time your driver asks you where you want to go you simply say: "I don't know. Wherever you want to go is fine with me." Then when your driver takes you to the place of his choice you complain and say: "I don't want to be here, take me somewhere else." And again you say you don't know where you want to go.

Can you see the confusion you would create? Can you see how you would never get to where you want to go because you haven't trained your driver to automatically take you where you want to go? You haven't given him the proper instructions.

Your mind and subconscious mind work the same way. If you don't train your mind to focus on your goals then your subconscious mind cannot create the situations that will help you achieve those goals. When you keep changing your mind, when you are not clear on what you want - your subconscious gets confused - and you end up exactly where you don't want to be.

Let's go back to the example of your personal driver. Wouldn't it be a lot easier and more comfortable if you told your driver where you wanted to go - or even better - your driver knew where you wanted to go ahead of time? But that will only happen when you train your driver by repeatedly telling him where you want to go on a regular basis.

Your subconscious mind is your driver. Your subconscious gets its instructions from your thoughts and beliefs. Give your subconscious the right instructions and it will take you where ever you want to go in life. When your mind is focused on your goals you direct your subconscious to create opportunities for you to achieve your goals. Your responsibility is to follow up on these opportunities.

How You Can Train Your Mind

Believe it or not I get a lot of calls and emails everyday from people who want to achieve their goals but simply can't get their mind to focus on the tasks that need to be done to have the success that they want. This happens because the mind is simply not used to focusing on your goals and following up with completing those tasks. So how do you get your mind to change? How do you train your mind?

106

The first step is to get the mind to stop doing what it is used to doing - or break the pattern that you've been following for so long. This will require some effort - but the reward will allow you to live the life you want and enjoy the level of success that you want.

To re-train your mind and direct your subconscious mind you start by paying more attention - so that when you see yourself getting distracted and not following up on things that you wanted to do - you take a step to break the pattern. You can break the pattern by doing something else. For example: you can start following up on what you had planned to do, you can create a list and follow up with it regularly to see if you are on track.

One thing that always works is to think about your goals every morning. As you're in bed, think about your goals and think about what you can do to achieve them during the day. If you find that you constantly say: "I don't know what do to do to achieve my goals." Then you're not looking for answers in the right place.

Take a look at what other people have done to achieve similar goals and see if you can follow the same process. For example: If you want to make more money take a look at someone else who has made a lot of money and see what they've done. Can you follow their process? Maybe you can even talk to them about the process? If you want to meet someone and be in a healthy relationship, talk to a friend who is in a successful relationship and find out what they did. By doing the above exercises you train your mind to focus on finding solutions while at the same time you direct your subconscious mind to create the opportunities for you to succeed. And - you begin to create a new pattern of thinking and you start to train the mind to work differently. You're now telling your driver where you want to go. This eliminates the confusion and allows you to achieve your goals.

You're not going to magically get your mind to focus or concentrate without you taking some form of action. When you finally do take some action your mind will still resist - but as you continue taking action the resistance will subside - REPITITION.

So what action can you take? First start with the exercise I just outlined above. Next - meditate. Meditation is one of the best ways to relax and calm your mind while training it to focus on what you want. When you meditate you actually start to clear the clutter that dominates your mind.

Make the Time

Finally it seems a lot of people have come to believe that they just don't have the time to achieve their goals. If you are one of the many who have such a belief then you've really convinced yourself that your goals are not worthy of your time; because if they were you would make the time for them. I'm not talking about spending an entire day or even a few hours. It's only a few minutes at different intervals. Why try to get everything crammed into one hour? Why not try to think about your goals at different intervals during the day? For example: you may have a few minutes while you're taking a walk - think of yourself achieving your goals. You could also do this while you're taking a shower, driving, walking, anytime. Here's a suggestion; the next time you are driving or taking a shower, pay attention to your thoughts. Are these thoughts actually working for your or against you? Would it be better to focus on your goals or keep recycling the negative clutter or junk in your head? The choice is yours - and taking action is really about taking a small step. You don't need to spend hours meditating. Even if you simply mediated for 5 or 10 minutes a day you'd be able to increase your ability to concentrate and focus by a 100-percent within a matter of days! Do it for weeks or months and you'll have dramatic results!

Our outer appearance changes as we age and move through life; are we born with a permanent self or can our identities be altered?

Human Growth

The Third Law of Thermodynamics – specifically the law of entropy - states that all of creation is winding down. Order is moving to chaos. As it applies to humans, we are born, grow until about the age of 22, then we begin to age (literally deteriorate) and eventually die. Look around you; some of us are deteriorating at a faster rate than others.

I'm 60 years old or 38-years into rot; how do I look? Oh, that hurt…okay I am over it!

From birth until approximately the age of 22, the body produces a hormone called HGH – human growth hormone. If you have ever watched children at play and heard the comment, "I wish I could bottle that energy and sell it, you would be bottling HGH!

By the age of 40, HGH secretion from the anterior lobe of pituitary gland is almost nil. Ageing accelerates quickly after the age of 40. There are two things that naturally stimulate HGH production – sleeping & strenuous exercise! Most of you are great at sleeping but not so great at strenuous exercise. You can thank me later for giving you a fantastic excuse for sleeping in to those people who accuse you of laziness.

My point is this: a good many factors of changing are out of our control but there are also a good many that we can control and this is where the most significant change must occur.

In Chapter 2, I outlined why and how you do the things you do. Subconscious belief systems acted upon by thought causes all action/conduct and behavior. It follows that in order to change, one needs to change their belief systems especially the ones that are causing the problems. These problems take the form of low self-esteem, low self-worth, depression, negative thinking and much more.

The healing begins in the actions that a person takes that I will describe below with the operative word being "actions".

The Central YOU Concept

Look at the picture below…

An observer will insert themselves in the picture by telling a story. This story is different between genders as well as maturity. But one essential common element of the story will be that it really has nothing to do with the woman; the story you would tell **yourself <u>is completely about you</u>**. This is called the "Central You" concept. All sensory input coming into your mind through the five senses are filtered and revolve around you. Most people live their lives with themselves at the center of their universe.

Now look at this picture…

This is another picture of a woman but this one is not real; it is an animated version. The story you would tell will be completely different or there would be no story at all. But if there were a story; it would also revolve around you because every fantasy you have is perfect where you are perfect too.

You are the idol of your fantasy!

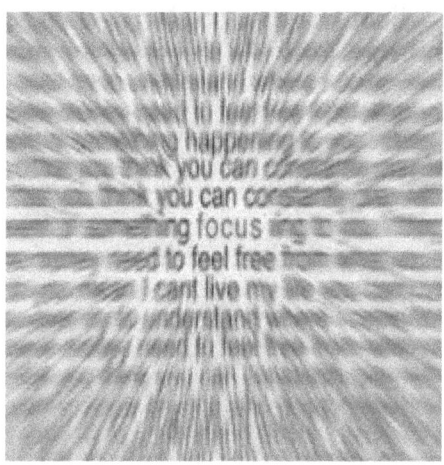

The Incredible Power of Focus

One important point to make is the idea that you really do create your own life and your own reality. Many people, after continuing to experience the same old ups and downs and personal dramas over many years, get to the point where they dismiss this idea as charming but useless -- or just plain wrong.

"If I'm creating this, then I'm certainly not doing it on purpose," they say. "It sure seems like this is HAPPENING to me, rather than that I'm creating it." They just assume that it's all BS because "this and this and this and this are going on for me, and I have no control over it, and anyone who thinks I'm creating this doesn't understand what I'm going through." Essentially, they are resigning themselves to becoming a victim of circumstances... the Central You!

We live in a universe of infinite complexity and many forces that operate on us -- way too many to keep track of. Yes, it is true that we are NOT in control of everything that happens because we are not in control of most of those infinite other parts of the universe. In fact, the only thing you have total and complete control over is YOUR OWN MIND; that is, if you learn how to exercise it.

Control over your mind gives you tremendous power. By exercising control over your mind, you can get the rest of those infinite other parts of the universe to begin to march in formation.

The person who says, "If I'm creating this, it certainly isn't on purpose," is right. They are not creating what is happening to them "on purpose." Who would purposely create failure, or bad relationships, or any other kind of suffering? You can only do something that is not good for you that is harmful to you, if you do it <u>subconsciously</u>. This means if you are creating something you don't want, you must be doing so subconsciously. Your mind is running on automatic pilot, based on the "software" (subconscious programming) installed when you were too young to know any better, by parents, teachers, friends, the media, and other experiences and influences. The key is to become more conscious, more aware...to get yourself off automatic pilot. Once you do this, you stop creating all the dramas and other garbage you don't want in your life.

How do you do this? One way is by remembering and using a very important piece of wisdom. What is this important piece of wisdom? I'm glad you asked...

Whatever you focus on manifests as reality in your life

You are always focusing on something, whether you are aware of it or not. If I spent some time with you, and heard your history, I could tell you what you are focusing on. How? By looking at the results you are getting in your life. The results are always the result of your focus. The problem is this focus is usually not conscious focus; it's automatic or subconscious focus. We subconsciously focus on something we don't want, and then when we get it we feel like a victim and don't even stop to think that we created it in the first place. We don't realize we could choose to create something completely different if we could only get out of the cycle of subconsciously focusing on something other than what we want.

Focusing on what you do not want, ironically, makes it happen. Focusing on not being poor makes you poor. Focusing on not making mistakes causes you to make mistakes. Focusing on not having a bad relationship creates bad relationships. Focusing on not being depressed makes you depressed. Focusing on not smoking makes you want to smoke. And so on. I think you get the idea. The mind will create what you focus on both GOOD and BAD!!!

Focusing the Mind

The truth is your mind cannot tell the difference between something you think about or focus on that you DO want, and something you think about or focus on but do NOT want.

The mind is a goal-seeking mechanism, and an extremely effective one at that. Already, all the time, it is elegantly and precisely creating exactly what you focus on. You are already a World Champion Expert at creating whatever you focus on. You couldn't get any better at it, and you don't need to get any better at it.

When you focus on anything, your mind says: "Okay, we can do that," and starts figuring out how to do it. It doesn't ask whether you're focusing on it because you want it or because you do not want it. It ALWAYS assumes you want what you focus on and then it goes and makes it happen. The more frequent and the more intense the focus, the faster and more completely you will create what you have focused on, which is why intense negative experiences create intense focus on what you do not want, and tend to make you re-create what you don't want, over and over.

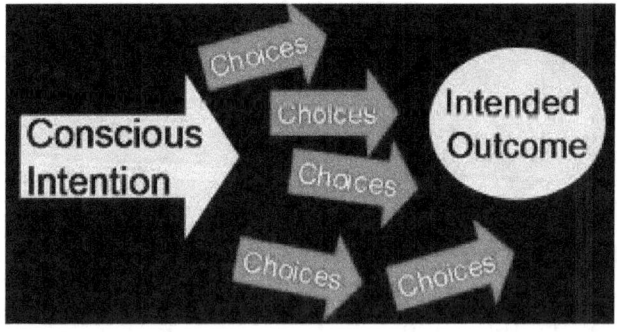

Conscious Intention

Most of the time, for most people, all the focusing and thinking is going by at warp speed, on automatic, without much, if any, conscious intention. Our job today is to learn how to direct this power by consciously directing your focus to the outcomes you want. Once you do, everything changes.

This does, however, take some work, because at first you have to swim upstream against the current of your old, unconscious habits, and the current can be swift and strong. Trained observation actually teaches you to focus on what you want.

First, you have to discover all the things you focus on that you do not want, and I'm willing to bet there are quite a few -- way more than you think. To the degree you're getting what you don't want, you are focusing, albeit subconsciously, on what you don't want.

Spend some time over the next few weeks making a list of all the things you do NOT want as you notice yourself thinking about them.

Second, you have to get very clear about what you DO want. Then, you have to examine each of the things you want and be sure they are not just something you do NOT want in disguise. For instance, saying "I want a relationship where I am treated well" would not even be an issue if you had not had relationships where you were not treated well, and even in making this seemingly positive statement you are focusing on not wanting to be mistreated. Saying "I want a reliable car" wouldn't even come up if you weren't focusing on the fact that you don't want a car that breaks down and needs a lot of repairs.

After you've sorted out the things you habitually focus on that you do not want, and know what you do want, you have to begin to notice each time you think about an outcome you do not want, and consciously change your thinking, right in that moment, so you're instead focusing on what you do want.

Remember, you do NOT have to avoid things to be happy and get what you want. The urge to avoid something is a result of having had a negative emotional experience regarding that thing, and trying to avoid things requires you to focus on them, which tells your brain to create them. Not good. You will be surprised how often you are thinking about what you do not want, how difficult it is to catch yourself doing it every time, and -- most of all – how difficult it is to switch your thinking to what you DO want.

The solution?

Practice, practice, practice. Persistence, persistence, persistence!!!

It's a very good idea to write down what you want, very specifically, so that your Fairy Godmother, were she to read it, would know exactly what to give you without any additional explanation.

Then, read what you have written to yourself, preferably out loud, several times a day, while seeing yourself, in your mind, already having what you want.

Believing is seeing and not the other way around as the world teaches you!

Another way to change your focus is to ask questions. As an example, I'll ask you one right now. What did you have for breakfast this morning? To answer this question (even to just internally process the question), you had to shift your focus from whatever your mind was focused on (hopefully, to what I am teaching) to today's breakfast.

This means that to change your focus, all you have to do is...ask yourself a question!

3-Steps to Controlling Your Mind

1. Awareness
The first step to changing anything is becoming aware that it's happening, especially if it's your mind. Pretend your mind is racing, and you finally realize that you're thinking. Most people at this stage get extremely frustrated and "try" to force their mind into submission. It doesn't work! Why? Because, what you focus on expands. The more frustrated you get, the more you're

119

focusing on frustration, so you'll get even MORE frustration and more thinking... on and on!

So the first step is to simply become "aware" of the fact that you're thinking. Nothing more. When you notice that you're thinking, smile to yourself, and say, "I just noticed myself thinking... interesting..." Now notice what happens inside of you when you do this... something VERY profound. If "I" just noticed "myself" thinking, perhaps there are really two completely separate identities running your life? There is the "I" and there is the "self."

The Power of Choice

The "I", is the real you...the intellect, the "I" behind the mind, that runs the show, the heart, the soul, the true conscious being, the choice maker.

The "self" is the desires, emotions and will of the mind; if left to run the show, it will run in endless circles until the edge of insanity.

The moment you do this, the moment you become "aware" - you are no longer a slave to your mind. You have won. After you become aware... do nothing, just lay there for 3 seconds and notice how it feels to be present in who you really are, not the mind, but you, the "I" -

there is a great feeling of peace behind that presence in the "I." Why?

Because when you are aware like this, you're aware of the power of your choice making. You now have the power of choice.

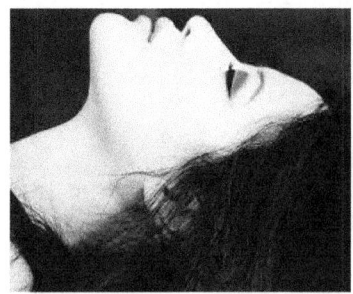

2. Relaxed Focus

"What you focus on expands." Now that you have become aware of your thinking, all you have to do is "direct" your mind into a place that will bring you into a deep, deep place of relaxation. Think about it, if before your mind will relentlessly race into any direction you give it; why not pick a direction that will give you peace and restful sleep? But, most people don't know what that direction really is. It's really easy. If you focus on anything your body does or feels subconsciously, you will begin to become more and more relaxed.

For example your breathing, the feeling of the pillow on your head, the sounds of nature outside (unless you live in the city), the warmth of your body. These are all things that happen, yet your conscious mind doesn't think about them. As you know, "What you focus on expands"... So what would happen if you focused on something that is happening in your "subconscious"? That's right, your conscious thinking would diminish, and your subconscious mind would begin to take over the entire process of you falling asleep! It really is that simple, and it works every time. The easiest one is your breathing. And I promise you if you just try this tonight, you will be shocked: "Wow! It worked!"

3. Repetition

Repetition
Repetition
Repetition

As I said, the easiest one to focus on is your breathing. In the beginning, you'll find this easier said than done. Begin by taking your focus onto your breathing. Take a deep breath in; hold it for a short while, slowly exhale. Count "1" Breathe in again; hold it shortly, exhale slowly, and count..."2". Why count? Because in the very beginning, you may find it challenging to hold your focus. In fact, you'll be surprised as you may not even make it to "5" the first time. This is because your subconscious ever-thinking mind will butt in and interrupt.

You may randomly go off into a barrage of thoughts again. If this happens, what do you do? Simply become aware, and begin focusing on your breathing again. As you become aware, 2 or 3 times, your mind will give up. When you get to "10" or "15" breaths you will feel a wave of relaxation in your body. This is the silent "click" as your mind shifts from the high frequency Beta brain-waves into Alpha brain-waves. Your subconscious mind will do the rest! The following exercise will teach you how to see and recognize things that are unworthy of attention, but still recognize that they are there. In other words, attention will be paid to it and then discarded CONSCIOUSLY.

I Have A Special Gift For My Readers

I appreciate my readers for without them I am just another struggling author attempting to make ends meet.

My readers and I have in common a passion for the written word as well as the desire to learn and grow from books.

My special offer to you is a massive ebook library that I have compiled over the years. It contains hundreds of fiction and non-fiction ebooks in Adobe Acrobat PDF format as well as the Greek classics and old literary classics too.

In fact, this library is so massive to completely download the entire library will require over 5 GBs open on your desktop.

Use the link below and scan all of the ebooks in the library. You can select the ebooks you want individually or download the entire library.

The link below does not expire after a given time period so you are free to return for more books rather than clog your desktop. And feel free to give the link to your friends who enjoy reading too.

I thank you for reading my book and hope if you are pleased that you will leave me an honest review so that I can improve my work and or write books that appeal to your interests.

Okay, here is the link…

http://tinyurl.com/special-readers-promo

PS: If you wish to reach me personally for any reason you may simply write to mailto:support@epubwealth.com.

I answer all of my emails so rest assured I will respond.

Meet the Author

Dr. Harry Jay is Director of Research for AppliedMindSciences.com, a mental health and mind research group of Applied Web Info, and is the author of over 100 books and research papers as a behavioral scientist.

In his 32-year career, Dr. Harry Jay has contributed many new mental health treatment treatments and protocols using some of the new advances he has discovered in Energy Psychology.

He specializes in addictions of all kinds, sexual abuse, child predation and gender relationships.

He is also a board member to ePubWealth.com and serves on the science committee assisting non-fiction science writers in book publishing and promotion.

As a leading behavioral scientist, he provides profiling services to the company's ForensicsNation.com unit as well as criminal psychology research to aid in identifying and apprehending child predators and cyber-criminals of all kinds.

He resides in Southern Utah and enjoys the outdoors, fishing and photography.

Visit some of his websites

http://www.AddMeInNow.com
http://www.AppliedMindSciences.com
http://www.BookbuilderPLUS.com
http://www.BookJumping.com
http://www.EmailNations.com
http://www.EmbarrassingProblemsFix.com
http://www.ePubWealth.com
http://www.ForensicsNation.com
http://www.ForensicsNationStore.com
http://www.FreebiesNation.com
http://www.HealthFitnessWellnessNation.com
http://www.Neternatives.com
http://www.PrivacyNations.com
http://www.RetireWithoutMoney.org
http://www.SurvivalNations.com
http://www.TheBentonKitchen.com
http://www.Theolegions.org
http://www.VideoBookbuilder.com